From Your Friends At The MAILBOX®

Mammals

Grades 1–3

INVESTIGATING SCIENCE

Project Manager:
Thad H. McLaurin

Writers:
Jan Brennan and Mary Sanford

Editors:
Cindy K. Daoust, Deborah T. Kalwat, Scott Lyons, Jennifer Munnerlyn, Leanne Stratton, Hope H. Taylor

Art Coordinator:
Clevell Harris

Artists:
Theresa Lewis Goode, Clevell Harris, Rob Mayworth, Barry Slate

Cover Artists:
Nick Greenwood and Kimberly Richard

www.themailbox.com

©2000 by THE EDUCATION CENTER, INC.
All rights reserved.
ISBN #1-56234-400-5

Except as provided for herein, no part of this publication may be reproduced or transmitted in any form or by any means, electronic or mechanical, including photocopying, recording, or storing in any information storage and retrieval system or electronic online bulletin board, without prior written permission from The Education Center, Inc. Permission is given to the original purchaser to reproduce patterns and reproducibles for individual classroom use only and not for resale or distribution. Reproduction for an entire school or school system is prohibited. Please direct written inquiries to The Education Center, Inc., P.O. Box 9753, Greensboro, NC 27429-0753. The Education Center®, *The Mailbox*®, and the mailbox/post/grass logo are registered trademarks of The Education Center, Inc. All other brand or product names are trademarks or registered trademarks of their respective companies.

Manufactured in the United States
10 9 8 7 6 5 4 3 2

Table of Contents

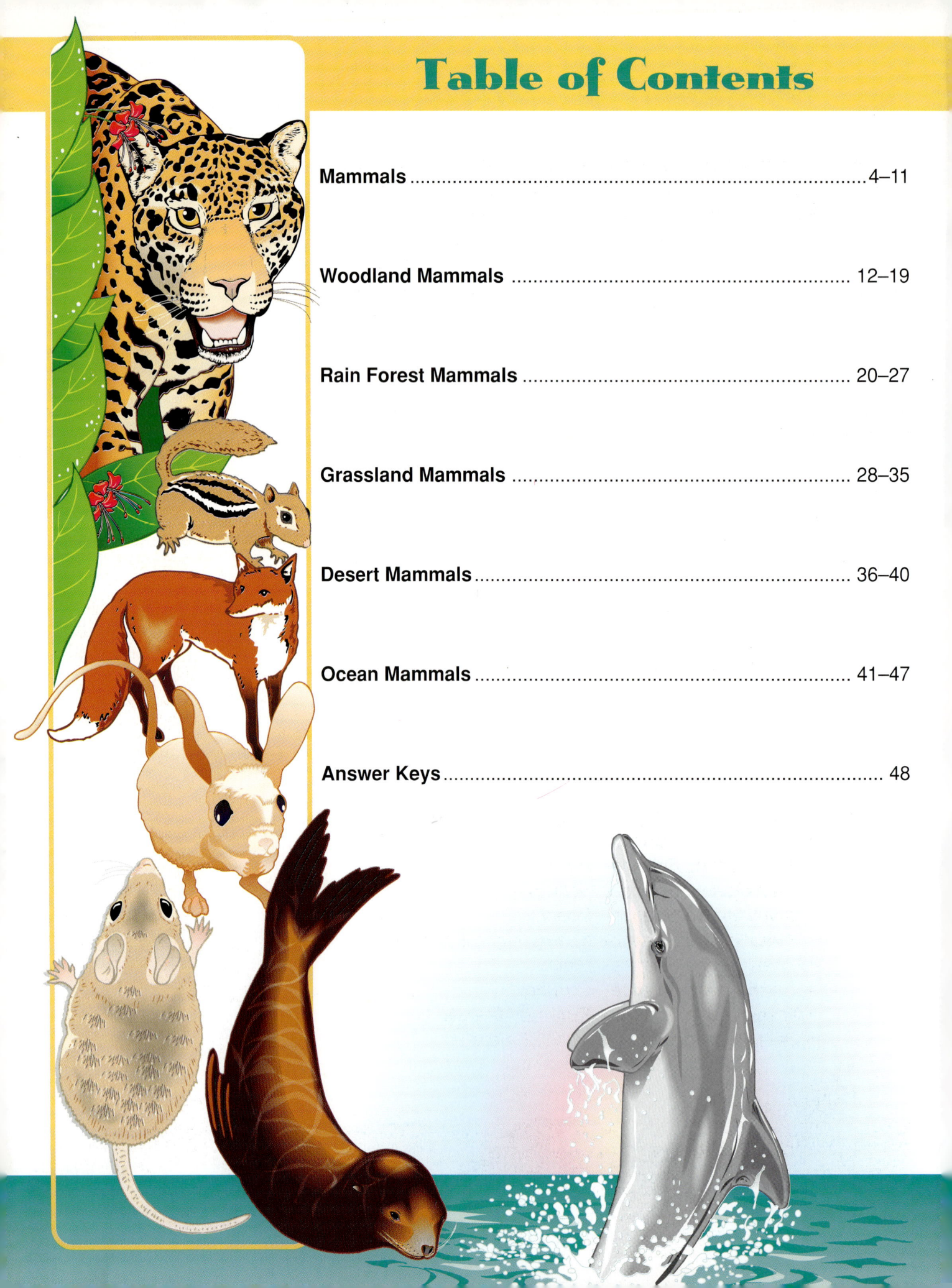

Mammals 4–11

Woodland Mammals 12–19

Rain Forest Mammals 20–27

Grassland Mammals 28–35

Desert Mammals 36–40

Ocean Mammals 41–47

Answer Keys 48

About This Book

Welcome to *Investigating Science—Mammals*! This book is one of ten must-have resource books that support the National Science Education Standards and are designed to supplement and enhance your existing science curriculum. Packed with practical cross-curricular ideas and thought-provoking reproducibles, these all-new, content-specific resource books provide primary teachers with a collection of innovative and fun activities for teaching thematic science units.

Included in this book:
Investigating Science—Mammals contains six cross-curricular thematic units each containing
- Background information for the teacher
- Easy-to-implement instructions for science experiments and projects
- Student-centered activities and reproducibles
- Literature links

Cross-curricular thematic units found in this book:
- *Mammals*
- *Woodland Mammals*
- *Rain Forest Mammals*
- *Grassland Mammals*
- *Desert Mammals*
- *Ocean Mammals*

Other books in the primary Investigating Science series:
- *Investigating Science—Amphibians & Reptiles*
- *Investigating Science—Environment*
- *Investigating Science—Solar System*
- *Investigating Science—Insects*
- *Investigating Science—Energy, Light, & Sound*
- *Investigating Science—Plants*
- *Investigating Science—Weather*
- *Investigating Science—Rocks & Minerals*
- *Investigating Science—Health & Safety*

Mammals

Use this collection of creative activities to introduce your students to the fascinating world of mammals.

It Must Be a Mammal
(Classifying)

It has hair, a backbone, and two pairs of limbs. It must be a mammal! Use the following activity to introduce your students to the major characteristics of mammals. Explain to your students that mammals have common characteristics including backbones, two pairs of limbs, and hair or fur. Further explain that mammal babies drink milk from their mothers. Provide each student with a copy of page 9. Guide students in reading each animal's name in the left-hand column and the four characteristics of mammals along the top of page 9. Direct students to mark an X in each box (to the right of each animal) that corresponds to a characteristic of that animal. Inform the students that an animal may have all, some, or none of the characteristics. If the animal has all four characteristics, it must be a mammal! Challenge your students to put other animals to the test. List other animals, both mammal and nonmammal, on the board. You'll be surprised how quickly your students will be able to sort out the mammals from the rest of the animals listed!

Background for the Teacher

- Mammals are members of the animal kingdom.
- Most mammals have hair or fur that serves many purposes. For some mammals, such as the tiger, fur or hair can help camouflage the animal from its prey or predators. A mammal's fur or hair can also provide heat control for the animal by keeping a layer of air close to its skin.
- Mammals feed their young on the mothers' milk.
- Mammals are also *vertebrates* because they have backbones.
- Mammals have two pairs of limbs. These arms, legs, or flippers suit the animal's needs for walking, running, swimming, or hanging.
- The lower jaw of a mammal is made of a single bone and can move without the rest of the head moving. The upper jaw is attached to the skull and can't move by itself. Because mammals can breathe while having food in their mouths, they are able to chew their food and don't have to swallow their food whole.
- Mammals are warm-blooded. Their body temperatures basically stay the same and aren't dependent on the surrounding temperatures.
- Most mammals give birth to well-developed young. Some mammals called *marsupials,* such as opossums and kangaroos, give birth to poorly developed babies, which then attach to their mothers' nipples and continue to grow. The nipples are usually located in a pouch on the mother's stomach. The platypus and the spiny anteater of Australia are very special mammals called *monotremes.* Both of these mammals lay eggs instead of giving birth to live young.
- There are around 4,500 types of mammals.
- The largest mammal is the blue whale. It can grow to be more than 100 feet long. The smallest mammal is the Kitti's hog-nosed bat. It's the size of a bumblebee.

Marvelous Mammal Readings

Amazing Animal Babies (Eyewitness Juniors No. 25) by Christopher Maynard (Alfred A. Knopf, Inc.; 1993)
Animal Senses: How Animals See, Hear, Taste, Smell and Feel by Pamela Hickman (Kid Can Press Ltd., 1999)
The Baby Zoo by Bruce McMillan (Scholastic Inc.,1995)
Cows Can't Fly by David Milgrim (Puffin Books, 2000)
Sam Who Never Forgets by Eve Rice (William Morrow and Company, Inc.; 1987)
What Is a Mammal? by Robert Snedden (Sierra Club Books for Children, 1993)

Home, Sweet Homes for Mammals
(Research, Classifying, Music)

Singing about animal habitats is a great way to teach your students about the places where mammals live and eat. Explain to your students that a *habitat* is a place where an animal naturally lives. Further explain that oceans, grasslands, deserts, woodlands, and rain forests are examples of animal habitats. Read the song shown below to your students and list on the board each mammal that is mentioned. Then divide students into five groups and assign a different verse (and habitat) to each group. Provide each group with one 12" x 18" sheet of construction paper, old magazines, crayons, scissors, glue, and appropriate reference books showing animals in their natural habitats. Instruct the group to find three facts about its assigned habitat and write the facts on the sheet of construction paper. Then have the group turn the sheet into a mini poster by adding illustrations and old magazine pictures of the mammals mentioned in its assigned verse. When each group has completed its poster, sing the song "What's a Habitat?" and have the children listen closely for their mammals. Then sing the song a second time, having each group raise its animal poster as its verse is sung. Soon all your students will feel at home with the five habitats.

Desert
The desert is dry. Desert mammals sleep during the day because it is so hot. The desert is sandy.

jackrabbit
kangaroo rat
coyote

What's a Habitat?
(sung to the tune of "Frère Jacques")

What's a habitat? What's a habitat?
Do you know? Do you know?
It's a place where animals naturally find space
To live and grow, to live and grow.

The ocean is a habitat. The ocean is a habitat.
Home for whom? Home for whom?
Walruses and seals, dolphins and whales
Are a few, are a few.

The desert is a habitat. The desert is a habitat.
Home for whom? Home for whom?
Mice, coyotes, and kangaroo rats
Are a few, are a few.

The grassland is a habitat. The grassland is a habitat.
Home for whom? Home for whom?
Elephants and zebras, lions and hyenas
Are a few, are a few.

The woodland is a habitat. The woodland is a habitat.
Home for whom? Home for whom?
Opossums, deer, and bobcats
Are a few, are a few.

The rain forest is a habitat. The rain forest is a habitat.
Home for whom? Home for whom?
Monkeys, sloths, and jaguars
Are a few, are a few.

The Race Is On!
(Comparing, Ordering)

Most mammals are active, but do your students know just how fast various mammals can move? This interactive bulletin board is a fun way to illustrate human speed compared to other mammals' speeds. Cover a bulletin board with green or blue paper. Then make a racetrack pattern (similar to the one shown) out of black construction paper and staple it to the center of the bulletin board. Next, make an enlarged construction paper copy of the mammal silhouettes on page 10. Place the hook side of 14 self-adhesive Velcro® squares around the racetrack. Cut the silhouettes into 14 separate cards. Then place the loop side of each Velcro square on the back side of each card. Record on a sheet of chart paper the information found in the Top Speed Chart on this page. Direct your students to compare the human speed to other mammal speeds shown on the chart. Have your students hypothesize why some mammals are faster and some are slower than humans. Then have student volunteers use the silhouette cards to arrange the mammals in order around the track with the slowest mammal near the starting line. Add to this bulletin board throughout your study of mammals by posting the speeds of other desert, woodland, ocean, rain forest, and grassland mammals as they are discovered by your students.

Top Speed Chart

Animal	Speed	Animal	Speed
Racehorse	45 mph	Bat	15 mph
Cheetah	70 mph	Sloth	1.3 mph
Rabbit	35 mph	Greyhound	40 mph
House Mouse	8 mph	Squirrel	12 mph
Gazelle	50 mph	Kangaroo	30 mph
Elephant	25 mph	Human	20 mph
Whale	20 mph	Dolphin	25 mph

Telltale Teeth
(Critical Thinking, Research, Making an Info Circle)

Sharpen your students' understanding of the different types of mammal teeth with this activity. Explain to your youngsters that there are different types of teeth, each designed with a different purpose. Tell your students that *canines* are sharp teeth used by *carnivores* to tear meat. *Molars* are flat back teeth used by *herbivores* to chew plants. Further explain that *incisors* are chisel-like front teeth used by mammals like the beaver for cutting through tough vegetable matter such as bark and stems. Explain that *omnivores*—animals that eat plants and meat—may need all three types of teeth. *Insectivores*, such as the shrew and the hedgehog, have teeth that help them eat insects. Tell your students that most mammals have at least two types of teeth. For example, they may have incisors for biting into food and molars for chewing the food. Have your students examine their own teeth and determine how many different types of teeth they have *(three: molars, incisors, canines)*. Then tell your students that some mammals—such as anteaters, sloths, and armadillos—are toothless.

Help your students brainstorm a list of mammal herbivores, carnivores, omnivores, and insectivores. Record the list on the board. (See sample list shown.) Next, have students work in pairs to complete the info circle on page 11. Give each pair a copy of page 11. Instruct the pair to select one mammal for each category of the info circle. Supply each pair with reference materials; then help the students research the types of foods eaten by each mammal as well as the type(s) of teeth of each mammal. Next, direct the pair to use its findings to complete each section of the infocircle. Schedule a time for each pair to share its findings with the rest of the class.

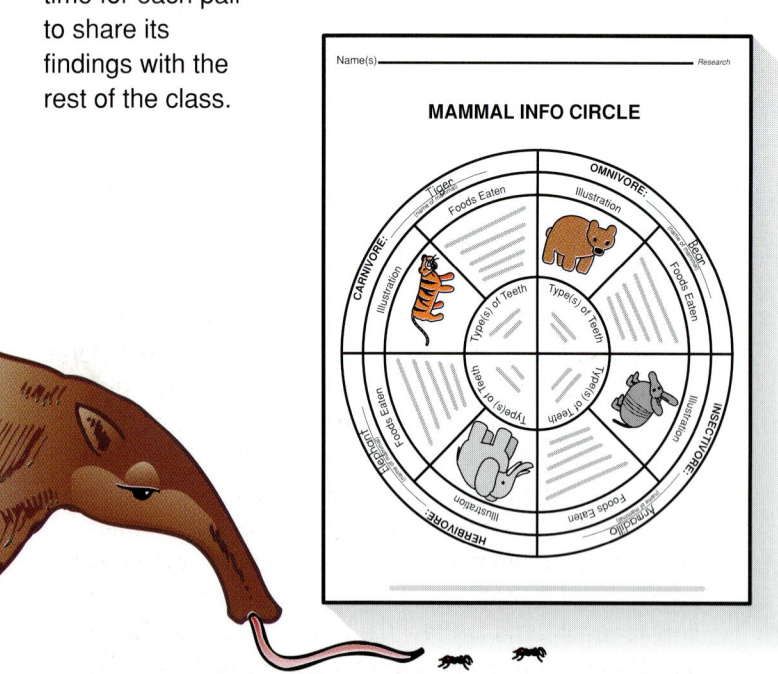

Herbivores	Carnivores	Omnivores	Insectivores
elephants	tigers	bears	shrews
giraffes	lions	raccoons	hedgehogs
beavers	wolves	humans	moles

Insectivore Delights
Mouthwatering bugs for our shrew, hedgehog, and mole guests!

Anthill Platter
A delightful array of delicious ants from around the world. Be quick! Try them all.

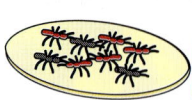

"Worm-ghetti"
Fat, skinny, long, and short worms served in mud gravy.

Termite Tickler
Fresh termites served on a warm bed of ants and spiders. Topped with diced worms!

Note from the chef: Eat at your own risk! Much of our food bites back!

Look Who's Coming to Dinner
(Creative Writing, Art)

Delight students with this marvelous mammal menu activity. Ask students to imagine opening a restaurant that caters to wild mammals. Tell your students that they are going to plan and create a menu offering tempting food to an array of mammals. Divide students into four groups and assign each group one mammal category: carnivores, herbivores, omnivores, or insectivores. Supply each group with one 12" x 18" sheet of construction paper, crayons or markers, and (if possible) sample restaurant menus. Instruct each group to think about the kinds of foods that would tempt mammals in its assigned category. Then have each group create one menu page listing several delicious meals for its special customers. Encourage students to be creative in describing and illustrating the foods on its menu page. (If provided, have the groups look at sample menus for layout ideas.) When the menu pages are complete, invite each group to present its page of delicious dishes to the class. Mount each menu page on a sheet of colored poster board. Display the menus on a wall space outside your classroom and then title the display "Magnificent Mammal Meals." Your class menu will delight and disgust all who read it!

What Am I?
(Writing a Riddle)

Mammal	Names
Adult	**Baby**
bear	cub
deer	fawn
elephant	calf
kangaroo	joey
leopard	cub
beaver	kit
goat	kid
pig	piglet
fox	pup
whale	calf
coyote	pup
sheep	lamb

Use the following fun riddle-writing activity to introduce your students to mammal baby names. In advance, make two or three enlarged copies of the adult and baby mammal names shown and one enlarged copy per student of the riddle template shown. Then cut each copy of the names into strips, making sure that each strip contains one adult mammal name and its corresponding baby name. Begin the activity by listing each mammal baby name on a sheet of chart paper. Have students guess, as you record on the board, the adult name for each baby. (Complete the chart with the adult names that students may not know.) Then give each student one strip, one copy of the riddle template, scissors, glue, and a sheet of construction paper. Tell each student to complete the riddle template with clues about the mammal baby on his strip. (Provide students with reference books on the various mammals listed if needed.) Once the student has completed his riddle, instruct him to fold the sheet of construction paper in half, cut out his riddle, and glue it to the front of the construction paper as shown. Direct the student to write the adult name of his mammal on the inside of the fold as shown. After each student has completed his riddle, have one student read his riddle to the class. Then instruct that student to call on another student to try to answer the riddle. If the answer is correct, the student who answered correctly reads her riddle to the class. If the answer is incorrect, the student reading his riddle calls on another student. Continue this process until each student has read a riddle. If desired, put the riddles in a center or post them on a bulletin board for students to continue to enjoy.

Baby Animal Riddle

I live in the _____.
   (habitat or where it lives)
I look like _____.

I eat _____.

I'm special because _____.
   (something unique about the animal)
When I'm a baby I'm called a _____.
   (baby name)
What am I?
©The Education Center, Inc.

Baby Animal Riddle

I live in the farm yard.
I look like fluffy balls of cotton.
I eat grass.
I'm special because I provide wool for clothes.
When I'm a baby I'm called a lamb.
What am I?

I am a sheep.

Mixed-Up Mammals
(Art, Creative Writing)

Tigeroo
(Tiger/Kangaroo)

Tammy the tigeroo spends part of the year in Australia and part of the year in India. She's a very beautiful animal. Tammy has orange and black stripes, pointed ears, and a long powerful tail that she often uses like an extra leg. She can hop really, really high, and she can run fast too. You can tell when she's happy by the purring sound she makes.
by Timmy

Stimulate your students' artistic abilities and their awareness of mammal body structure by creating pictures of mixed-up mammals. To begin the activity, have students brainstorm a list of mammals as you record them on the board. Tell students to read over the list and choose two mammals. Then instruct each student to combine the physical characteristics of both mammals into one new mammal. Supply each student with drawing paper, crayons, and picture books of mammals. Allow time for each child to draw her unique imaginary mammal. When the pictures are complete, have each child name her new mixed-up mammal. Then have her write a short story about her creation, telling what the animal can do with its combined features. Culminate the activity by having the students read their stories to each other in pairs. If desired, display the completed illustrations and stories on a bulletin board titled "Mixed-Up Mammals."

How Long Is a Lifetime?
(Math, Making a Timeline)

If all mammals celebrated their birthdays, some would have an amazing number of candles on their cakes! Use this hands-on timeline activity to involve students in comparing various mammals' average life spans. In advance, make a transparency of the life span chart shown. Then provide each student with one 5" x 8" index card and crayons. Instruct each child to draw and color a birthday cake on her card. Next, display the life span chart transparency and assign one animal to each student. Have each student write her assigned animal's name and life span on the card below the illustrated birthday cake. Then guide students in arranging themselves in order from the shortest to the longest animal life span by asking questions such as, "Who thinks their mammal has the fewest birthdays?" "Who thinks their mammal has the greatest number of birthdays?" "Whose mammal's total number of birthdays is more than five but less than seven?" Continue asking similar questions until all the students are standing around the room in sequential order. Culminate the activity by hanging a clothesline across the room and having each student clip her birthday cake card to the line in order from shortest to longest life span.

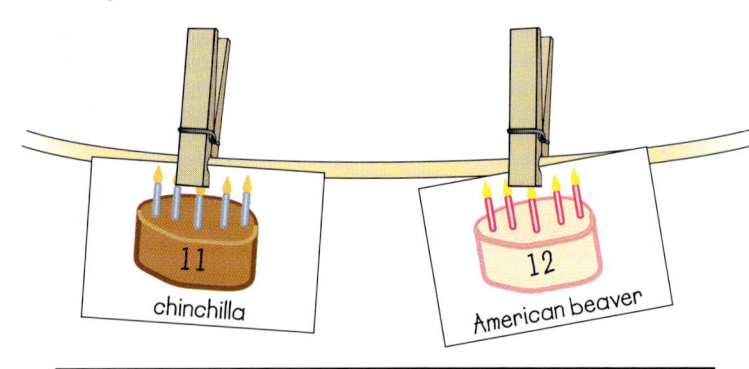

Mammal Life Span Chart

rabbit	18 years	aardvark	23 years
house mouse	1 year	guinea pig	8 years
tiger	20 years	horse	20–30 years
African elephant	65 years	gorilla	50 years
blue whale	45 years	American beaver	12 years
golden hamster	3–4 years	bottle-nosed dolphin	25 years
giraffe	28 years	killer whale	60 years
squirrel	10–12 years	platypus	17 years
chinchilla	11 years	giant panda	26 years
coyote	21 years	walrus	17 years
American bison	33 years	kangaroo	6–8 years
lion	15–20 years	hippopotamus	30 years
Indian rhinoceros	49 years	Bactrian camel	35 years

Life-Giving Lungs
(Making a Model, Experiment)

Give your youngsters a look inside mammal breathing with this simple model. Explain to students that mammals have special organs that help them breathe: two *lungs* and a *diaphragm*. Further explain that the diaphragm is a dome-shaped muscle that is attached to the ribs and helps the lungs move air in and out. Tell your students that they are going to build models to illustrate how the diaphragm moves down (during inhalation) to make more room in the lungs for air and moves up (during exhalation) to push the air out of the lungs. Then follow the steps below to help each student create his model.

After each student has completed his model, have him predict what will happen when he lightly pushes the stretched balloon *(the diaphragm)* at the base of the bottle. *(The two small balloons that represent the lungs will deflate.)* Explain that this occurs because the stretched diaphragm pushes the air in the bottle against the small balloons, forcing the air contained in each to leave through the straw. Then have your students predict what will happen when they release the stretched balloon. *(The two small balloons will reinflate with air.)* Explain that as the diaphragm relaxes, the lungs are able to expand and refill with air.

Materials for each student: one 8-oz. plastic water bottle, 1 straw cut in half, 3 elastic bands, 2 small balloons, 1 large balloon, small lump of clay

Steps:
1. Ahead of time, cut about one inch off the water bottle's bottom. Slit each large balloon up one side.
2. Have students assist one another in stretching the large slitted balloon over the bottle's bottom and securing it with an elastic band.
3. Direct each student to fit one smaller balloon over each end of each straw half, securing both balloons with elastic bands.
4. Have each student insert the two straws through the top of the bottle, stopping when the balloons are about one inch from the large balloon base. Then have him seal the hole around the straws with the clay.

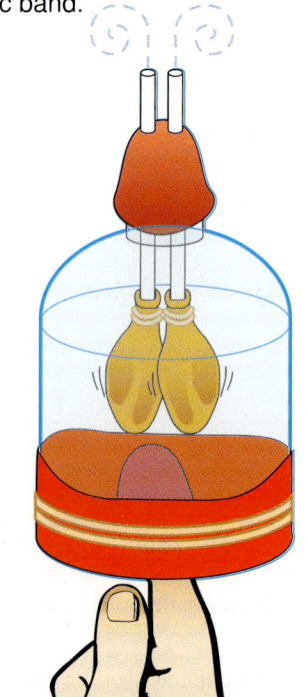

Name _____ *Identifying characteristics of mammals*

It Must Be a Mammal

		Does it have hair or fur?	Does it have a backbone?	Does it have two pairs of limbs?	Does it drink milk from its mother?
horse					
grizzly bear					
earthworm					
elephant					
rabbit					
spider					
kangaroo					
chicken					
grasshopper					
human					

Bonus Box: On the back of this paper, list the animals that are not mammals. Then choose one and write a sentence telling how you know it is not a mammal.

©2000 The Education Center, Inc. • *Investigating Science* • Mammals • TEC1742 • Key p. 48

Note to the teacher: Use with "It Must Be a Mammal" on page 4.

Patterns
Use with "The Race Is On!" on page 5.

racehorse 45 mph	cheetah 70 mph	rabbit 35 mph	house mouse 8 mph
gazelle 50 mph	elephant 25 mph	whale 20 mph	bat 15 mph
sloth 1.3 mph	greyhound 40 mph	squirrel 12 mph	kangaroo 30 mph
human 20 mph	dolphin 25 mph		**Start**

Names _____ Research

MAMMAL INFO CIRCLE

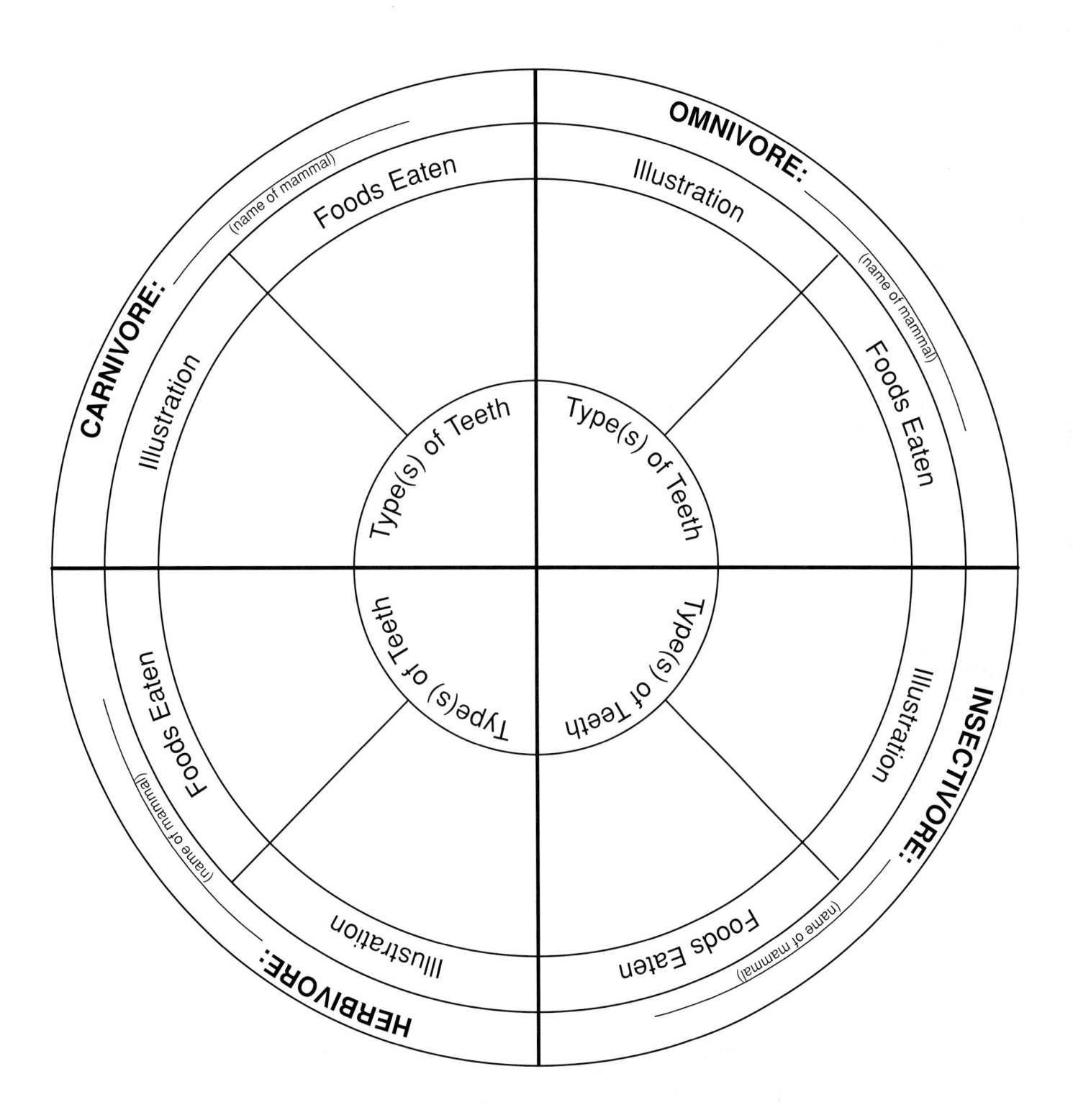

CARNIVORE: _____ (name of mammal)
- Foods Eaten
- Illustration
- Type(s) of Teeth

OMNIVORE: _____ (name of mammal)
- Illustration
- Foods Eaten
- Type(s) of Teeth

HERBIVORE: _____ (name of mammal)
- Foods Eaten
- Illustration
- Type(s) of Teeth

INSECTIVORE: _____ (name of mammal)
- Illustration
- Foods Eaten
- Type(s) of Teeth

©2000 The Education Center, Inc. • *Investigating Science • Mammals* • TEC1742

Note to the teacher: Use with "Telltale Teeth" on page 6.

11

Woodland Mammals

Introduce your students to the wonderful world of woodland mammals with the following activities and experiments.

Background for the Teacher

- The woodlands of the United States, Canada, and most of Mexico are *temperate forests*.
- Many woodland mammals—such as the chipmunk, fox, and woodchuck—have small bodies so they can move easily in the underbrush.
- Other woodland mammals like the bear, deer, and moose are quite large.
- The shores of ponds and lakes provide shelter and food for some woodland mammals that live on both land and in water, such as the beaver, muskrat, and otter.
- Many woodland mammals are hunted by humans for food and for their valuable fur.
- Woodland mammals are often a source of enjoyment. People visit national parks to view them in their natural environments.
- Woodland mammals are important in the balance of nature because they promote plant growth. For example, their droppings fertilize the ground, as well as contain seeds from plants the mammals have eaten; nuts buried by squirrels often sprout into trees; burrowing mammals dig up the soil—enabling air, moisture, and sunlight to break down soil.
- Woodland mammals have well-developed senses of hearing and smell, but many are color-blind.
- Woodlands contain mammals that are *herbivores* (beavers), *carnivores* (wolves), *insectivores* (bats, shrews), and *omnivores* (bears, opossums).
- Bats are the only mammals that can fly.
- Some woodland mammals (such as the beaver) live in social groups, which offer protection from predators and allow sharing of food.

Woodland Homes
(Brainstorming, Assessing Previous Knowledge)

Introduce students to woodland mammal homes with this activity. In advance, make a transparency of the simple woodland scene shown. (Use transparency pens to color the scene if desired.) Display the transparency so that all your students can see the woodland scene. Point out to your students the various areas of a woodland—the tree, the stream and pond, the cave, and the underground section. Explain to your students that a woodland is the natural *habitat* for many mammals. Then ask students to brainstorm a list of different woodland mammals. Record the mammal names on the transparency according to where students think the mammals' homes are located. For example, woodchucks and rabbits live in underground homes and beavers and otters often live near streams and ponds. Periodically revisit the transparency throughout your study of woodland mammals and have your students reevaluate the location of each mammal name. Make any needed corrections and add any additional mammals discovered by students. At the end of your unit, make a photocopy of the transparency for each student to color and keep as a reference.

Woodsy Tales

All About Deer by Jim Arnosky (Scholastic Inc., 1999)
In the Woods: Who's Been Here? by Lindsay Barrett George (Mulberry Books, 1998)
Temperate Forests (Eco Zones) by Lynn M. Stone (Rourke Enterprises, Inc.; 1989)
In Woods & Forests by Tessa Paul (Crabtree Publishing Co., 1997)
Think of a Beaver by Karen Wallace (Candlewick Press, 1995)

Order ID: 104-3347930-6048247

Thank you for buying from Susie's Teacher Books on Amazon Marketplace.

Shipping Address:
Scott Gandolfe
41 Somerset Ave
Bridgewater, NJ 08807

Order Date: Sep 19, 2012
Shipping Service: Standard
Buyer Name: Scott Gandolfe
Seller Name: Susie's Teacher Books

Quantity	Product Details
1	Mammals: Grades 1-3 (Investigating science series) [Unknown Binding] [2000] Bren... Merchant SKU: 7Z-X3WF-LG0N ASIN: 1562344005 Listing ID: 0607M89GKMH Order-Item ID: 33141106499226 Condition: New

Returning your item:
Go to "Your Account" on Amazon.com, click "Your Orders" and then click the "seller profile" link for this order to get information about the return and refund policies that apply.
Visit http://www.amazon.com/returns to print a return shipping label. Please have your order ID ready.

Thanks for buying on Amazon Marketplace. To provide feedback for the seller please visit www.amazon.com/feedback. To contact the seller, please visit Amazon.com and click on "Your Account" at the top of any page. In Your Account, go to the "Orders" section and click on the link "Leave seller feedback". Select the order or click on the "View Order" button. Click on the "seller profile" under the appropriate product. On the lower right side of the page under "Seller Help", click on "Contact this seller".

Home, Sweet Home
(Researching, Completing a Chart)

Your students will dig in to learning some of the different names for woodland mammal homes. In advance, make an enlarged copy of the chart at right. Then duplicate the enlarged copy to make a half-class set. Divide your students into pairs and give each pair one copy of the chart. Supply the class with a variety of reference materials and picture books on woodland mammals. Then direct each pair to place a check mark in the appropriate box for each mammal on the chart to show what type of home it builds. (For some animals, more than one box may be checked) Have two pairs swap completed charts to check each other's research. (See answer key on page 48.) Have students save their completed charts to use with the activity "At Home in the Woods" on this page.

	Wooded Area	Den	Nest	Burrow	Tunnel	Hollow Tree	Lodge
Bear							
Porcupine							
Skunk							
Fox							
Squirrel							
Chipmunk							
Rabbit							
Marmot							
Woodchuck							
Mole							
Mouse							
Deer							
Beaver							
Opossum							
Raccoon							
Marten							
Otter							
Muskrat							

Steps 1, 2, 3

Step 4

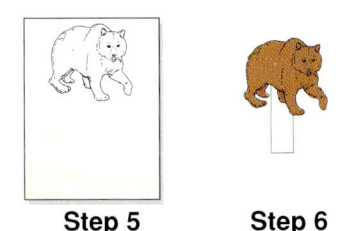

Step 5   **Step 6**

Step 7

At Home in the Woods
(Making a 3-D Habitat Model)

After having your students complete the "Home, Sweet Home" chart on this page, have them continue to work in pairs to create a 3-D woodland mammal habitat model. Instruct each pair of students to choose several different animals from the "Home, Sweet Home" chart to include in its habitat. Then guide each pair through the steps below to create its 3-D model. After completing its 3-D model, have each pair write a brief description of its habitat and the mammals that live there. Have each pair share its model and written description with the rest of the class. Then display the models in the library for other classes to learn from and enjoy.

Materials for each pair:
one 9" x 12" sheet of white construction paper
1 copy of page 18
2 to 3 index cards
ruler
crayons
scissors
tape
glue

Steps:
1. Use a ruler and pencil to measure and mark a two-inch border on three sides of the construction paper as shown.
2. Draw a picture of a woodland scene to match the homes of the animals chosen. Use crayons to color the scene. (For example, if a pair has chosen a bear, raccoon, and rabbit from the chart, its woodland scene should include a cave for the bear, a tree for the raccoon, and an underground burrow for the rabbit.)
3. Cut a two-inch slit up from the bottom of the construction paper along the right and left margins, to form two tabs as shown.
4. Fold the bottom border up; then pull the left and right tabs underneath the folded middle section and secure them with tape, forming a three-sided display box.
5. Cut out the selected woodland mammals illustrated on page 18 along the bold cut lines. Glue each illustration onto an index card, leaving plenty of space below it as shown.
6. Color and carefully cut out each animal shape around the outline of the illustration, leaving a one-inch tab at the bottom of the illustration as shown.
7. Fold back the tab on each cutout. Place a small dab of glue on each tab; then glue each cutout to the appropriate area on the woodland scene, creating a 3-D effect as shown.

13

Camouflage Capers
(Creative Thinking, Art)

Use the following activity to blend factual information and fun as your students discover how some woodland animals use camouflage to hide from predators and prey. Begin by reading aloud *What Color Is Camouflage?* by Carolyn Otto (HarperCollins Children's Books, 1996). After reading the book, explain to your students that animals use their coloration, color pattern, and/or shape to blend into their natural backgrounds and disguise themselves from predators as well as prey. Have students help you list the mammals from the book that might be found in a woodland (deer, skunk, mice, marmots, foxes). Next, have your students discuss the various ways they use camouflage. Then give each student a copy of the rabbit pattern on page 17 and crayons or markers. Next, ask the student to select an area of the classroom—such as a desk, the carpeting, or the wall— where she can hide her rabbit. Have each student color her rabbit pattern to match the selected area. Then have her cut out the rabbit and use tape to mount it in that area. Challenge classroom visitors to find the hidden rabbits!

Black and White All Over
(Comparing, Contrasting)

Help your students envision a world without color as they focus on woodland animal eyesight. In advance, ask volunteers to donate several rolls of black-and-white and color film. To begin, explain to your students that many woodland mammals are color-blind. Then take your students outside and allow them to assist you in taking a black-and-white picture and a color picture of several different objects or people. After the film has been developed, display the photos and have your students compare each set of pictures. Direct them to compare the differences in shadows, texture, and detail of each picture. Finally, add the sets of pictures to a bulletin board titled "Black-and-White Sight."

Keeping Track
(Making a Class Field Guide, Research)

Your students will know for sure which animal has crossed their paths after creating a class woodland mammal tracks guide. In advance, make one copy of page 17 for each pair of students, making sure to mask the rabbit pattern at the bottom of the page. Next, gather reference books and nonfiction books for student research, such as *Whose Tracks Are These?* by Jim Nail (Roberts Rinehart Publishers, 1996). Then divide students into pairs and guide each pair through the steps below to create its page for the tracks guide. After each pair has completed each step and created its page of the field guide, use three rings to assemble all the pages into one field guide. Once the guide has been completed, read each set of clues to your students and challenge them to guess which animal belongs to each set of tracks. Keep the booklet in the classroom as a reference guide for your students.

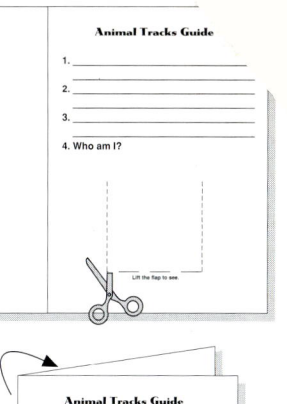

Step 1

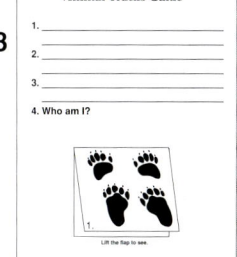

Steps 2, 3

Materials for each pair:
1 copy of the booklet page on page 17
1 mammal illustration square from page 18
1 matching animal track square from page 19
glue
scissors

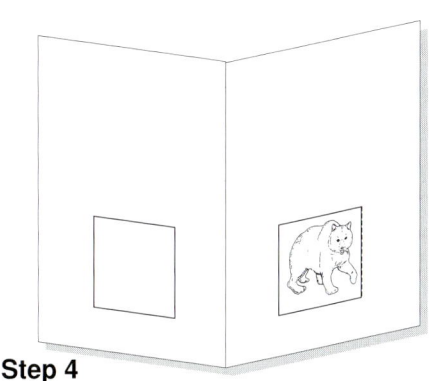

Steps:
1. Cut along the dotted lines of the square on the booklet page to create a flap.
2. Glue the animal track square on top of the flap.
3. Fold the booklet page in half along the fold line.
4. Glue the mammal illustration square on the inside folded page, as shown, so that it shows through when the flap on the outer page is lifted.
5. Glue both sides of the folded page together as shown.
6. Write three facts as clues on the lines provided (such as the size, eating habits, type of home, color, seasonal habits).
7. Hole-punch the booklet page along the left side.

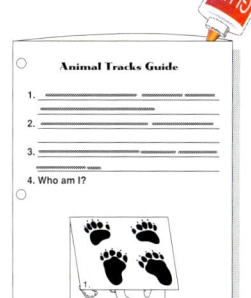

Step 4

Steps 5, 6, 7

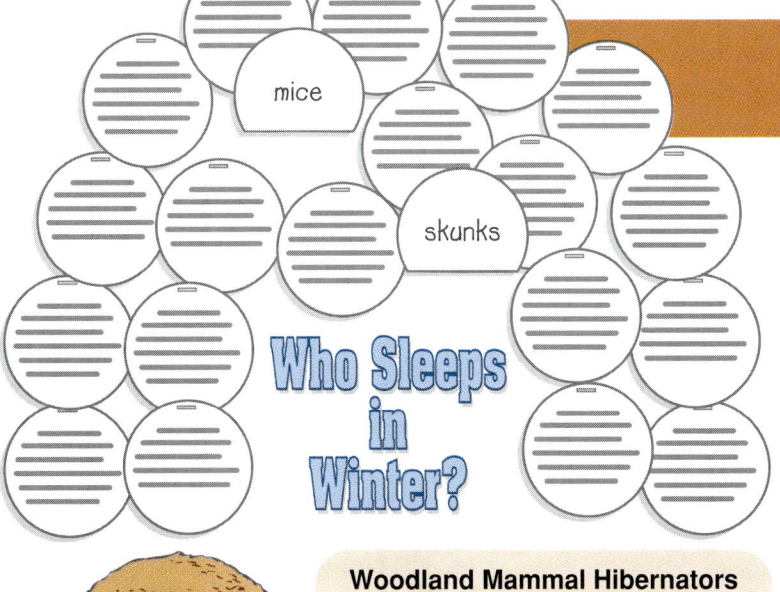

Who Sleeps in Winter?
(Research and Writing, Bulletin Board)

Awaken your students' interest in woodland hibernators with this research activity. Begin by explaining to your students that many mammals hibernate (go into a deep sleep) during the winter. Next, have pairs of students research one hibernating woodland mammal (see list below) to find the answers to the following questions: Does it sleep continuously or awaken to eat? Will a loud noise awaken it? Does its body change? Where does it choose to hibernate? Why does it awaken in the spring? Instruct each pair to record each question on a circle of white construction paper, without revealing the mammal's name. Instruct the pair to write the mammal's name upside down on the back of the circle (toward the bottom). Display, on a bulletin board, all the completed circles in the shape of a snow cave as shown. Use only one staple at the top of each circle so that it can be flipped up to reveal the name of the hibernating mammal being described.

Woodland Mammal Hibernators

bats	mice
bears	opossum
chipmunks	skunks
hamsters	squirrels
hedgehogs	woodchucks
marmots	

All Ears
(Listening Experiment)

Your students will be all ears as they complete the following experiment. In advance, gather one windup kitchen timer. Then explain to students that many woodland mammals depend on their keen senses to help them survive. Many mammals have physical features, such as larger ears, to intensify the usefulness of their senses. Further explain that some mammals' hearing is sensitive enough to detect the squeak of a mouse in a meadow or an insect crawling on a piece of grass. To begin the experiment, have students sit in a circle on the floor, and ask one student to wind up and hide the timer as the other students close their eyes and cover their ears. Ask students to remove their hands from their ears and listen carefully for the ticking timer. Then instruct each student to point (without opening her eyes) in the direction of the ticking sound. Next, have each student hold one hand cupped around each ear. Wind up the timer again and have the students listen with their ears cupped. Ask your students if it is easier or harder to hear the ticking timer with their ears cupped (easier). Point out to your students that cupping your ears simulates an animal's large ears. Further explain that cupping their ears increases the clarity of the sound similar to the way an animal's larger ears provide it with keen hearing. Repeat the experiment several times, allowing a different student to hide the clock each time.

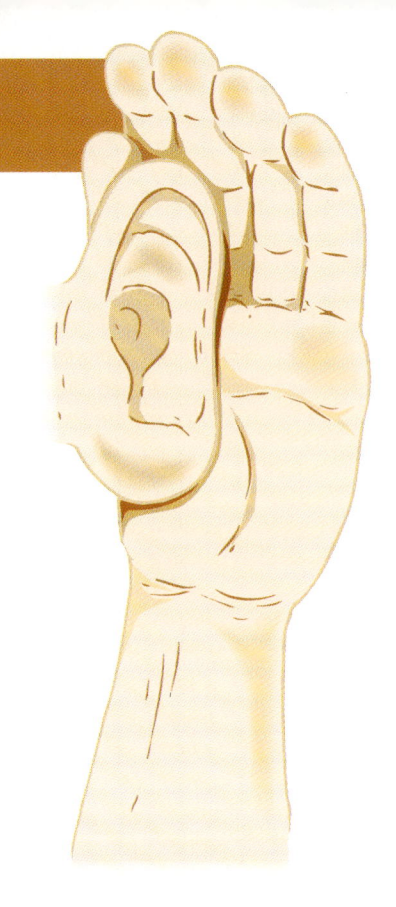

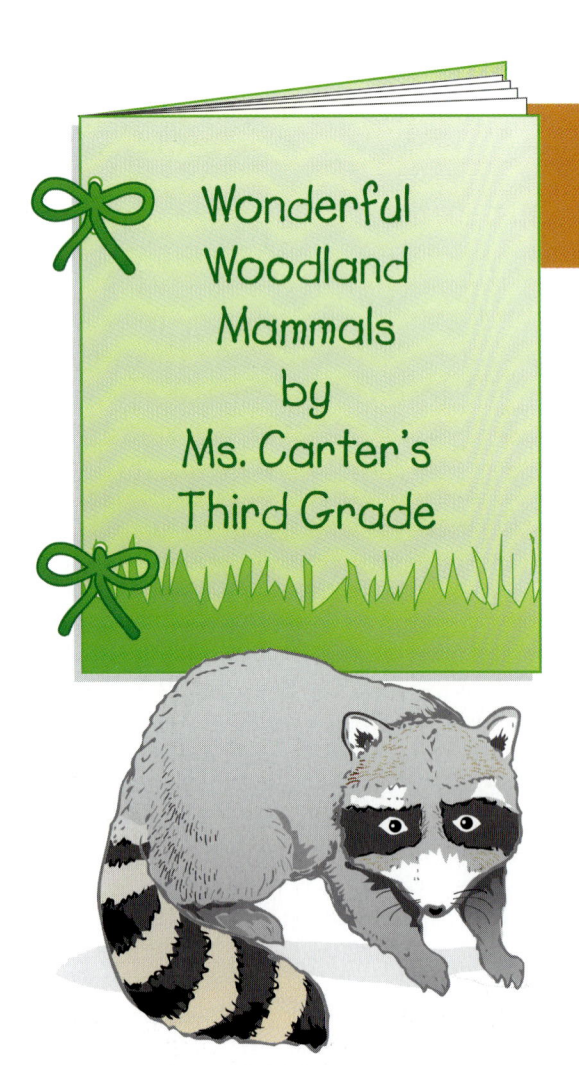

Wonderful Woodland Mammals
(Researching, Making a Picture Book)

Culminate your study of the woodland mammal's way of life by creating a woodland mammal picture book. Assign each student in your class one of the mammals listed below. Provide each student with a sheet of white drawing paper, crayons or markers, and access to reference books on mammals. Write the following questions on the board for each student to research on his assigned mammal: Is it a carnivore, herbivore, insectivore, or omnivore? Where does it live? Is it active at night or during the day? Instruct each student to illustrate on the sheet of drawing paper a picture of his assigned mammal. Then direct the student to research the three questions and write the answer to each question below the illustration of the mammal. After each student has completed his page, gather all the pages and stack them in ABC order by the name of each mammal. Have a few students design a cover for the book with the title "Wonderful Woodland Mammals." Then use a hole puncher and yarn to bind the cover and stack of illustrations into one book. (If available, use a bookbinder to give the book a more professional look.) Send the book home each night with a different student to share with his family.

Woodland Mammals

bear	opossum	otter	hedgehog
beaver	rabbit	muskrat	moose
chipmunk	raccoon	mink	wolf
deer	skunk	marmot	shrew
fox	squirrel	marten	bat
porcupine	woodchuck	mole	mouse

Animal Tracks Guide

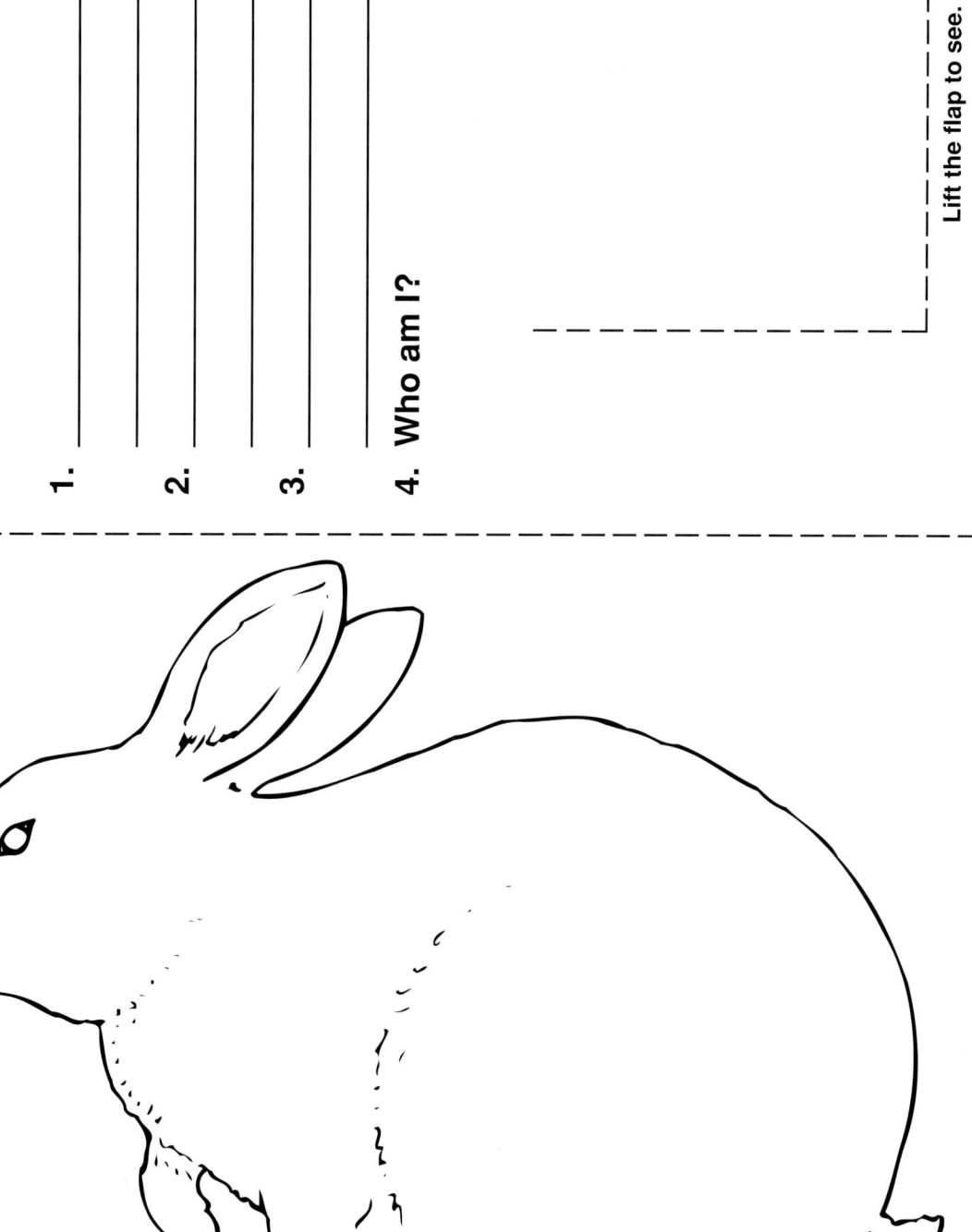

1.
2.
3.
4. Who am I?

Lift the flap to see.

©2000 The Education Center, Inc. • *Investigating Science* • *Mammals* • TEC1742

©2000 The Education Center, Inc. • *Investigating Science* • *Mammals* • TEC1742

Note to the teacher: Use the booklet page with "Keeping Track" on page 15. Use the rabbit pattern with "Camouflage Capers" on page 14.

Patterns
Use with "At Home in the Woods" on page 13 and "Keeping Track" on page 15.

1. bear	2. beaver	3. chipmunk
4. deer	5. fox	6. porcupine
7. opossum	8. rabbit	9. raccoon
10. skunk	11. squirrel	12. woodchuck

18　　©2000 The Education Center, Inc. • Investigating Science • Mammals • TEC1742

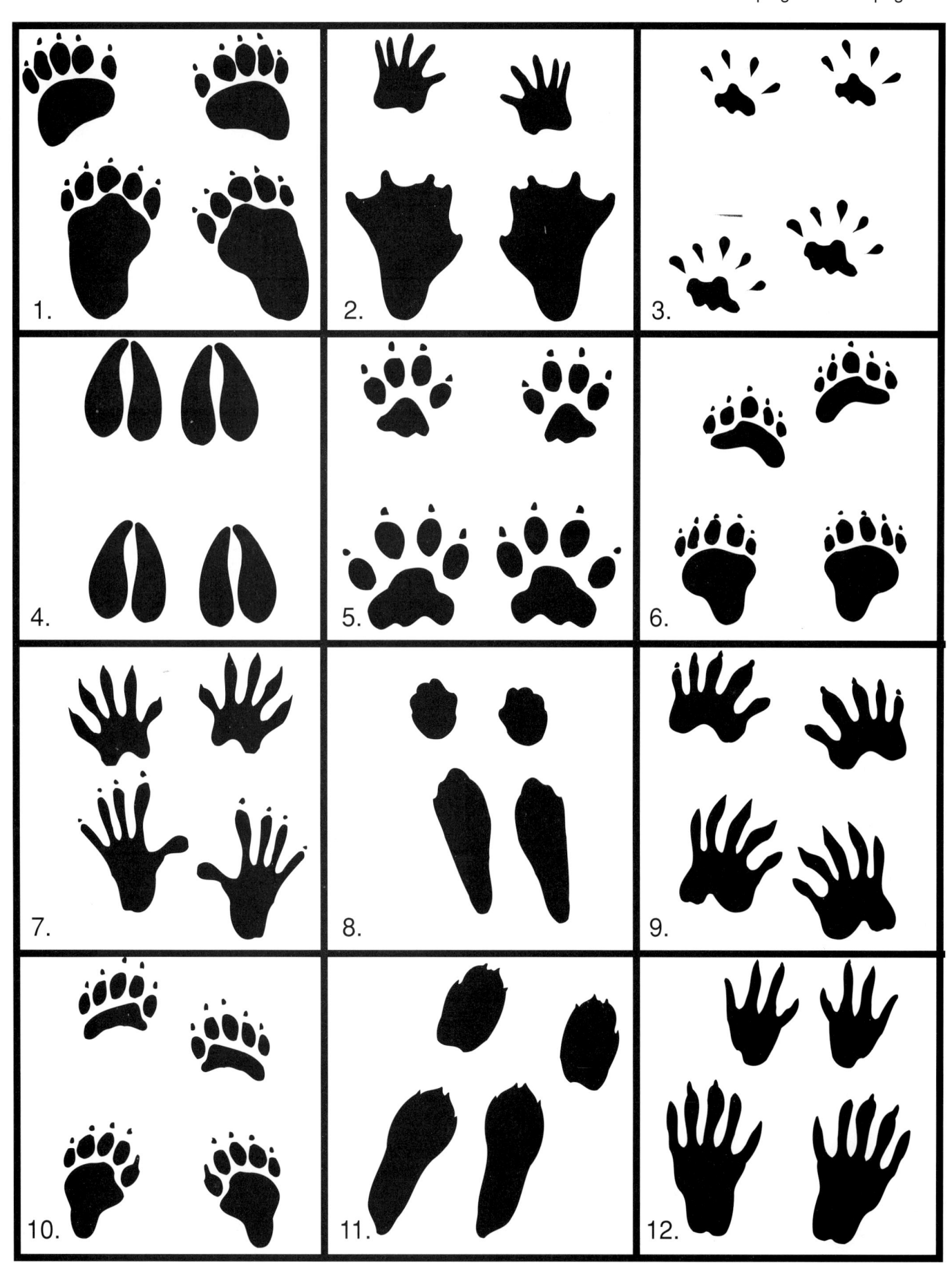

Animal Track Squares
Use with "Keeping Track" on page 15.

Rain Forest Mammals

Prepare your students for an exciting adventure as they explore rain forest mammals with the following activities and reproducibles.

Where in the World?
(Classifying, Listening)

Here's a fantastic way to familiarize your students with the different rain forest areas while practicing classifying and listening skills. Begin by explaining to students that there are three main rain forests in the world: African, Asian, and South American. Use a map or globe to show your students each continent and its proximity to the equator. Further explain that all rain forests have similar hot, humid climates because they are close to the equator, but different types of plants and animals live in each forest. Use the following activity to help each child learn about the types of mammals living in each rain forest. Distribute a large sheet of construction paper, a copy of page 24, glue, and scissors to every student. Help the student divide his paper into three sections and label it as shown. Next, have each student cut apart the mammal pictures on page 24 and use the code to help him glue each picture under the correct heading on the construction paper. Then read aloud each rain forest mammal fact shown on this page as the student points to the animal on his page. Finally, have your students discuss the similarities and differences between the mammals found in the three rain forests.

Background for the Teacher

- Tropical rain forests are located around the equator in an area called the *tropics*.
- Rain forests are hot (68–95°F) and wet (about 60–80 inches of rain annually) year-round.
- Over half of the world's known plant and animal species are found in the rain forests.
- Many mammals, such as monkeys and sloths, spend their lives in the trees in the rain forest.
- Larger rain forest mammals, such as deer and antelope, search for food along the rain forest floor.
- Both *herbivorous* (plant-eating) and *carnivorous* (meat-eating) mammals live in the rain forest.

Rain Forest Mammal Facts

African Rain Forest:
The **chimpanzee** is very intelligent. It is the only mammal, besides man, that can recognize itself in a mirror.
The **flying squirrel** is 20 to 33 inches long and can glide up to 300 feet from tree to tree.
The male **gorilla** can weigh up to 450 pounds. All gorillas stand and walk resting on their knuckles.
The **okapi** is a member of the giraffe family and weighs as much as a pony.
The **pangolin** uses its 27-inch tongue to catch and eat termites and ants. Sharp pointy scales cover its body.

Asian Rain Forest:
The **orangutan** has a flat face and a reddish beard. It likes to climb slowly through the trees, using its feet like another set of hands to grasp branches.
The **Malayan tapir** is the size of a pony, but it looks more like an elephant. It moves quickly, making trails through the forest.
The **slow loris** is about 12 inches long and has short ears, a short tail, and huge staring eyes. It moves slowly from branch to branch eating fruit at night.
The **Philippine tarsier** has large orange-tinted eyes and a small face. It leaps from branch to branch catching insects to eat.
The **Sumatran tiger** is a fairly small warm-weather tiger. Today only a few hundred Sumatran tigers live on the island of Sumatra.

South American Rain Forest:
The **jaguar** looks like a big leopard. It can weigh up to 200 pounds. It is a good climber and swimmer.
The **kinkajou** is part of the raccoon family. It is also known as a honey bear because it likes to hook its tail on a branch and hang upside down eating the honey from bees' nests.
The **ocelot** is a small cat with a beautifully marked coat. It is the only cat that sleeps like a dog by resting its head on its stretched-out forepaws.
The **golden lion tamarin** is a rare but beautiful monkey. A long golden mane covers its head and shoulders.
The **giant armadillo** is the biggest of all armadillos. It eats termites, ants, worms, and snakes. It has about twice as many teeth as other mammals.

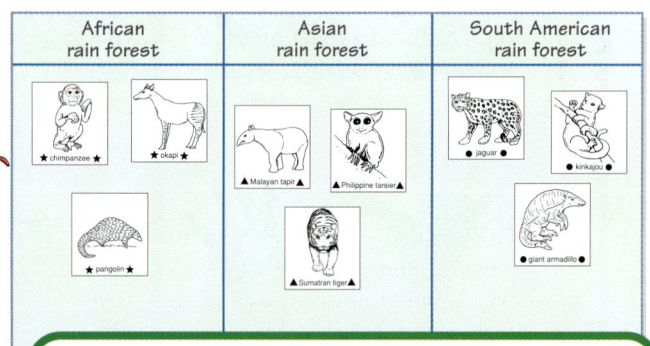

Roaring Rain Forest Reads

Anansi and the Talking Melon by Eric A. Kimmel (Holiday House, Inc.; 1995)
The Chimpanzee Family Book by Jane Goodall (North-South Books Inc., 1997)
How to Babysit an Orangutan by Tara Darling (Walker Publishing Company, Inc.; 1996)
In the Forest With the Elephants by Roland Smith (Gulliver Books, 1998)
Very First Things to Know About Monkeys by Sarah Albee (Workman Publishing Company, 1999)
What Is a Bat? by Bobbie Kalman (Crabtree Publishing Company, 1998)

Telling Trunks
(Making a Model, Writing)

Why do elephants have such long trunks? Help your students answer this question and learn more about the world's largest land mammals with this fact-filled activity. Explain that there are two types of elephants: *Asian* and *African*. Further explain that Asian elephants are smaller than African elephants. They also have smaller ears and only one lump, called a *lobe,* on the end of their trunks instead of two. Tell your students that an elephant uses its trunk in the same way a person uses his hands, lips, nose, and facial muscles. Help each student make an elephant fact trunk by providing him with the materials listed; then guide each student through the directions below. Supply students with reference books on elephants and instruct them to find the various ways elephants use their trunks. Have students share their findings while you record them on the board. Then have each student write at least eight elephant trunk facts on his trunk as shown. For younger students, write on a sheet of chart paper the list of trunk facts below. Then have the students write the facts on their trunks as you read each fact aloud. As a follow-up activity, allow each student to wear his trunk while you read aloud the classic tale *Elephant's Child* by Rudyard Kipling (Harcourt Brace & Company, 1988).

Materials for each student: (Ahead of time prepare several tagboard trunk-shaped tracers.) two 12" x 18" sheets of gray construction paper, two gray pipe cleaners, scissors, stapler, single-hole puncher

Directions:
1. Trace the trunk shape onto each sheet of construction paper; then cut out each trunk.
2. Staple the two trunk shapes together along both sides, leaving the ends open.
3. Punch one hole (through both thicknesses) in the middle of the larger end of the trunk. Secure one pipe cleaner through each hole.
4. Place the wide end of the trunk over your nose; then fit the pipe cleaners around your ears.

Trunk Facts:
1. It's an all-purpose tool.
2. It can draw up water like a straw.
3. It can be used for a spray bath.
4. It can pick up and move objects.
5. It can be used to hug or discipline other elephants.
6. It can wipe an elephant's eyes.
7. It helps reach food.
8. It is used to smell and to test food.

Night Vision
(Experiment, Writing)

Use this quick experiment to shine some light on the habits of nocturnal rain forest animals. Begin by telling students that a rain forest is as busy at night as it is during the day. Many nocturnal animals, like the African bush baby, sleep throughout the day and then wake up to search for food at night. Further explain that some *nocturnal* animals can see especially well at night because they have large eyes. Their pupils widen to let in more light than animals with smaller eyes, allowing them to see better in the dark. Use this quick experiment to show your students how the size of a pupil changes due to the amount of light. Pair students. Direct each pair to sit facing each other and look at (not touch) each other's pupils (the black center portion of the eye). Have each partner take turns closing her eyes, then quickly opening them as her partner watches her pupils. The pairs will notice that their pupils are quite large but quickly shrink when exposed to the light. To follow up this activity, provide each child with a copy of the top half of page 25. Have each child cut out and color her bush baby paper topper and glue it to the top of a sheet of lined paper as shown. Instruct the child to write a story about what it might be like to be a nocturnal animal living in the rain forest at night.

If I were a bush baby in the rain forest, I'd be able to see really well at night. Because I'd be nocturnal, I'd get to stay up all night long!

Meg

Be Batty
(Reading, Making a Model)

Let your students get a little batty with this high-flying activity. Begin by reading aloud *Stellaluna* by Janell Cannon (Harcourt Brace & Company, 1993). With students' help list similarities and differences between bats and birds. (For example: They both can fly. However, bats are mammals, giving birth to live young that they nurse. Birds hatch from eggs and do not nurse their young.) Next, explain to students that bats are the only flying mammals. Further explain that most of the 900 different types of bats live in the tropics because they can find food year-round. The scientific name for bats, *Chiroptera,* means "hand-wing." To demonstrate how a bat's wing resembles a human hand, show an enlarged copy of each bat wing pattern shown. (Enlarge until the span of each wing is about 12 inches.) Point out to students the "fingers" found in the bat's wing. Have each student make a hand-wing bat model. Provide each student with the materials listed; then guide the student through the directions below.

Materials for each student: two enlarged copies of each wing pattern shown, one 18-oz. Styrofoam® cup, one 3" Styrofoam® craft ball, 10 black pipe cleaners, black or brown tempera paint/glue mixture (1 part Elmer's® glue to 2 parts paint), 1 paintbrush, 2 black jelly beans, 1 red gumdrop, 3 toothpicks, 2 wiggle eyes, glue, scissors, tape

Directions:
1. Paint the cup and the craft ball with the paint/glue mixture. Set aside to dry.
2. Cut out all four wing patterns. Pair and glue two wings together so that the white lines (bones) show on each side of the wing.
3. Cut each pipe cleaner to match the length of each white line on the front of one wing pattern. Tape each pipe cleaner to the appropriate bone on the pattern. (Leave extra pipe cleaner for each upper arm bone as shown.)
4. Carefully insert the extra *upper arm* pipe cleaner through the side of the cup as shown. Secure the pipe cleaner inside the cup with tape.
5. Repeat Steps 3 and 4 to construct the other wing.
6. Carefully stick each black jelly bean on the end of a toothpick. Then insert the other end of each toothpick into the top of the craft ball as shown. Repeat the process with the remaining toothpick and the gumdrop to add a nose to the craft ball as shown.
7. Glue the wiggle eyes onto the craft ball; then place a line of glue around the rim of the cup and sit the ball in the cup as shown.

Animal Antics
(Critical Thinking, Writing)

Why are students fascinated by animals? Because the animals' actions sometimes remind them of their own. Use the following creative-writing activity to give your students a chance to see that they have some things in common with rain forest mammals. To begin, have each child choose a favorite rain forest mammal from the list below. Then have the child research her animal to find any attributes or actions they might have in common. Have the student write a sentence describing how she and the animal are similar; then have her draw a picture of herself performing an action similar to one her chosen rain forest animal would perform. Encourage each student to share her sentence and picture with the class. Compile all of the sentences and pictures into a class book titled "How We Are Like Our Rain Forest Friends."

Rain Forest Mammals:
sloth
chimpanzee
jaguar
bush baby
leopard
anteater
tiger
bat
elephant
gorilla

Sometimes I'm as slow as a sloth.

Monkey Business
(Research)

Students will love learning about Old and New World monkeys and their habitats with this activity. Begin by asking your students if they know the difference between *apes* and *monkeys*. Explain that apes—chimpanzees, gibbons, gorillas, and orangutans—do not have tails. Apes are also expert climbers. Monkeys do have tails and usually run, jump, and leap along the branches of trees. Further explain that the 200 species of monkeys are divided into two categories: *Old World monkeys* and *New World monkeys*. Use the information below to make a chart listing the characteristics of Old and New World monkeys; then discuss these characteristics with your students. Next, assign each child an Old or New World monkey to research. Make a copy of the bottom half of page 25 for each student. Direct the student to use encyclopedias, library books, and other resource materials to color the checklist on his "Monkey Business Card." Instruct each student to draw a picture of his monkey in the space provided on the card. Set aside time for each youngster to present his research to the class. Display the business cards on a bulletin board titled "Monkey Business Is Serious Business!"

New World monkeys
- They are found in the tropical forests of Central and South America.
- They have nostrils that point sideways and are far apart, called "flat noses."
- Some have *prehensile* tails, or long, useful tails that can hold onto branches.
- Most have 36 teeth.
- All New World monkeys live in trees.

(capuchin monkeys, howler monkeys, ouakaris, sakis, spider monkeys, squirrel monkeys, woolly monkeys, marmosets, tamarins)

Old World monkeys
- Most are found in the tropical forests of Africa and Asia.
- They have nostrils that are close together and face downward, called "down-facing noses."
- They cannot hold onto branches with their tails, and some have very small tails.
- Most have 32 teeth, like humans do.
- Many Old World monkeys live on the ground.

(baboons, colobus monkeys, guenons, langurs, macaques)

Monkey Business Card

Old	New	is found in Africa or Asia
Old	New	has a small tail
Old	New	has 36 teeth
Old	New	has a long, useful tail
Old	New	lives up in the trees
Old	New	has a "down-facing nose"
Old	New	has 32 teeth, like humans do
Old	New	has a "flat nose"
Old	New	is found in Central or South America
Old	New	sometimes lives on the ground

Spider Monkey
(Name of Monkey)

is a __New__ World Monkey

(Monkey Picture)

"Purrr-fect" Rosettes
(Analyzing, Comparing, Art)

Can you tell a leopard from a jaguar? Your students will be able to after completing the following fun activity. Explain to your students that leopards and jaguars are the largest cats found in the rain forest. Both cats are spotted rather than striped. The spots help camouflage the cats. Further explain that leopards and jaguars look similar, but have some important differences. On a sheet of chart paper, list the differences shown below. Then read and discuss these differences with your students. Next, display a transparency of the cat spots shown. Explain to students that the easiest way to tell the two cats apart is by looking at their *rosettes* (spots). Have your students describe the differences in the leopard and jaguar rosettes. Point out that leopards have small empty rosettes, while jaguars have larger rosettes with one or more dots in the center. Have students make rosette T-shirts to show what they've learned. Have each child bring a clean, white T-shirt to class. Provide every child with a black permanent marker and a piece of cardboard (about 11" x 14"). Instruct each child to insert the cardboard inside the shirt. Then display the transparency of the two types of rosettes. Have each student use the marker to write "Leopard" on the front of the T-shirt and "Jaguar" on the back. Next, direct the student to draw leopard rosettes on the front of the shirt and jaguar rosettes on the back. Culminate the activity by scheduling a day for everyone to wear their T-shirts to school and explain to their peers and other teachers the difference between the two types of rosettes.

leopard:
- lives in Africa and Asia
- is smaller than a lion or a tiger
- has a longer tail, a lighter body weight, and a smaller head than a jaguar

jaguar:
- lives in Mexico and Central and South America
- is usually larger than a leopard
- has a shorter tail and a heavier body than a leopard
- has a big head, short legs, and big paws relative to its body size

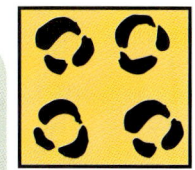

leopard

jaguar

For more fun activities on rain forest mammals, see "Forest Dwelling" on page 26 and "Jungle Stats" on page 27.

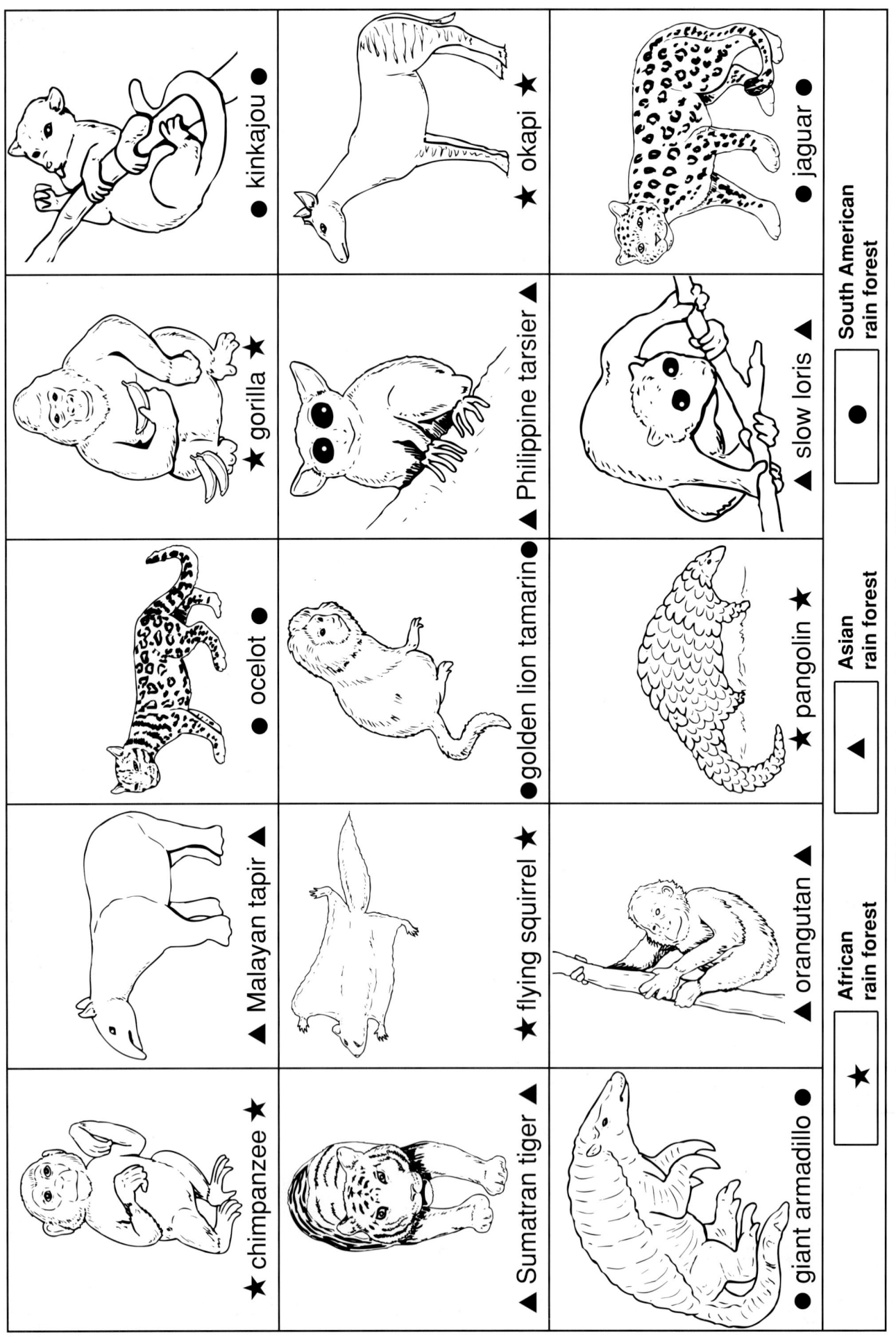

★ chimpanzee	▲ Malayan tapir	● ocelot	★ gorilla	● kinkajou
▲ Sumatran tiger	flying squirrel ★	● golden lion tamarin	▲ Philippine tarsier	★ okapi
● giant armadillo	▲ orangutan	★ pangolin	▲ slow loris	● jaguar

★	▲	●	
African rain forest	Asian rain forest	South American rain forest	

©2000 The Education Center, Inc. • *Investigating Science • Mammals* • TEC1742

Note to the teacher: Use with "Where in the World?" on page 20.

Pattern
Use with "Night Vision" on page 21.

©2000 The Education Center, Inc. • *Investigating Science • Mammals* • TEC1742

Use with "Monkey Business" on page 23.

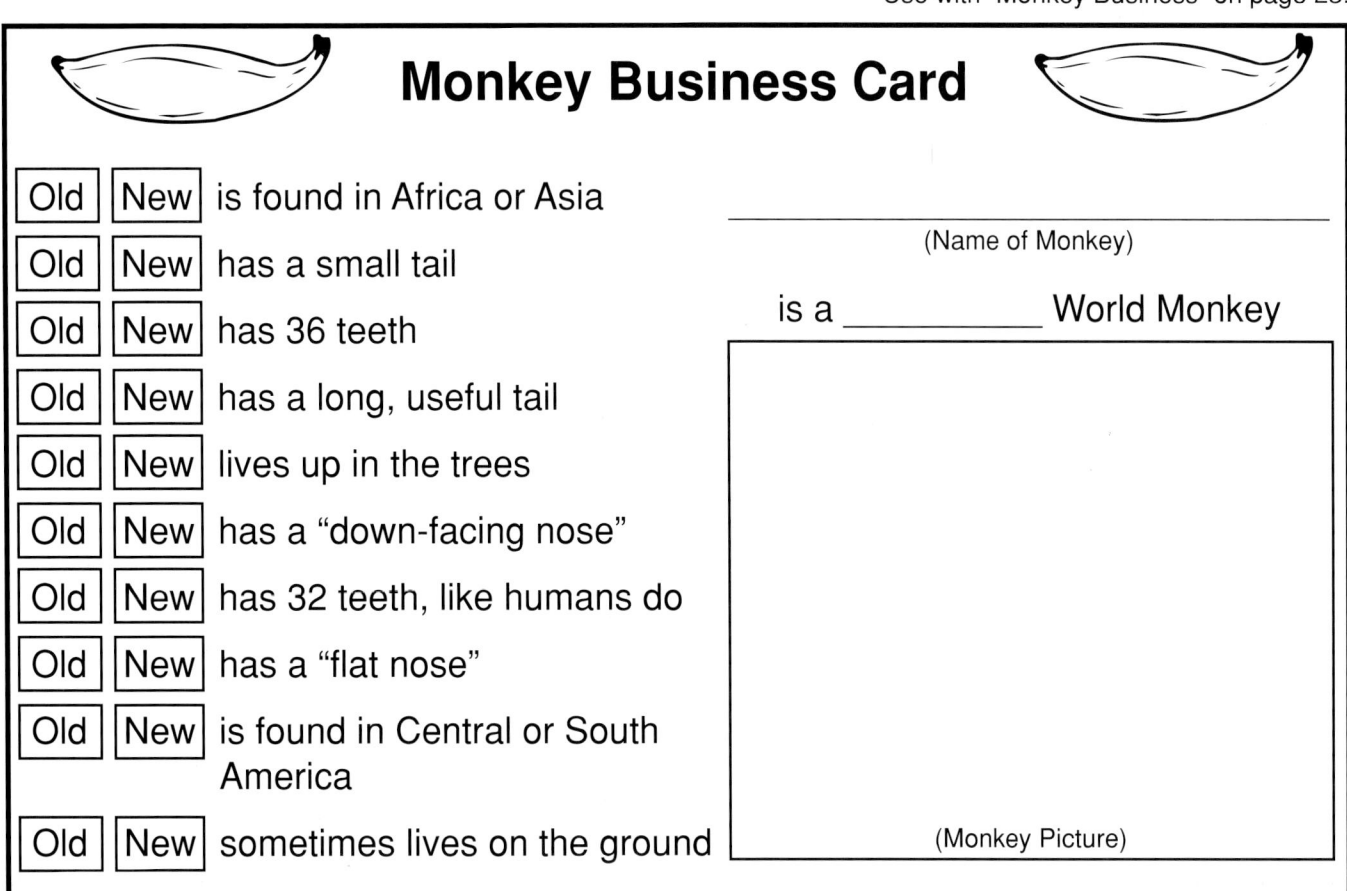

Monkey Business Card

Old	New	is found in Africa or Asia
Old	New	has a small tail
Old	New	has 36 teeth
Old	New	has a long, useful tail
Old	New	lives up in the trees
Old	New	has a "down-facing nose"
Old	New	has 32 teeth, like humans do
Old	New	has a "flat nose"
Old	New	is found in Central or South America
Old	New	sometimes lives on the ground

_____
(Name of Monkey)

is a _____ World Monkey

(Monkey Picture)

©2000 The Education Center, Inc. • *Investigating Science • Mammals* • TEC1742

Name _____

Forest Dwelling

Many different mammals *dwell*, or live, in the rain forest. Some live high up in the trees, while others stay on the forest floor. Cut out the mammal pictures to the right. Read the information in each box; then use a dot of glue to glue each picture in the correct spot.

spider monkey | giant anteater | leopard | sloth | gorilla | capybara

- I hang upside down at the top of the forest.
- I shuffle along the forest floor searching for food.
- I only climb up here to reach fruit, to get a better view, or to sleep.
- I like to rest on branches.
- High up in the trees, I move very quickly from limb to limb.
- I like to eat plants from streams in the rain forest.

Bonus Box: Choose one of the animals above. On the back of this paper, write a few sentences describing what a day in the forest might be like for that animal.

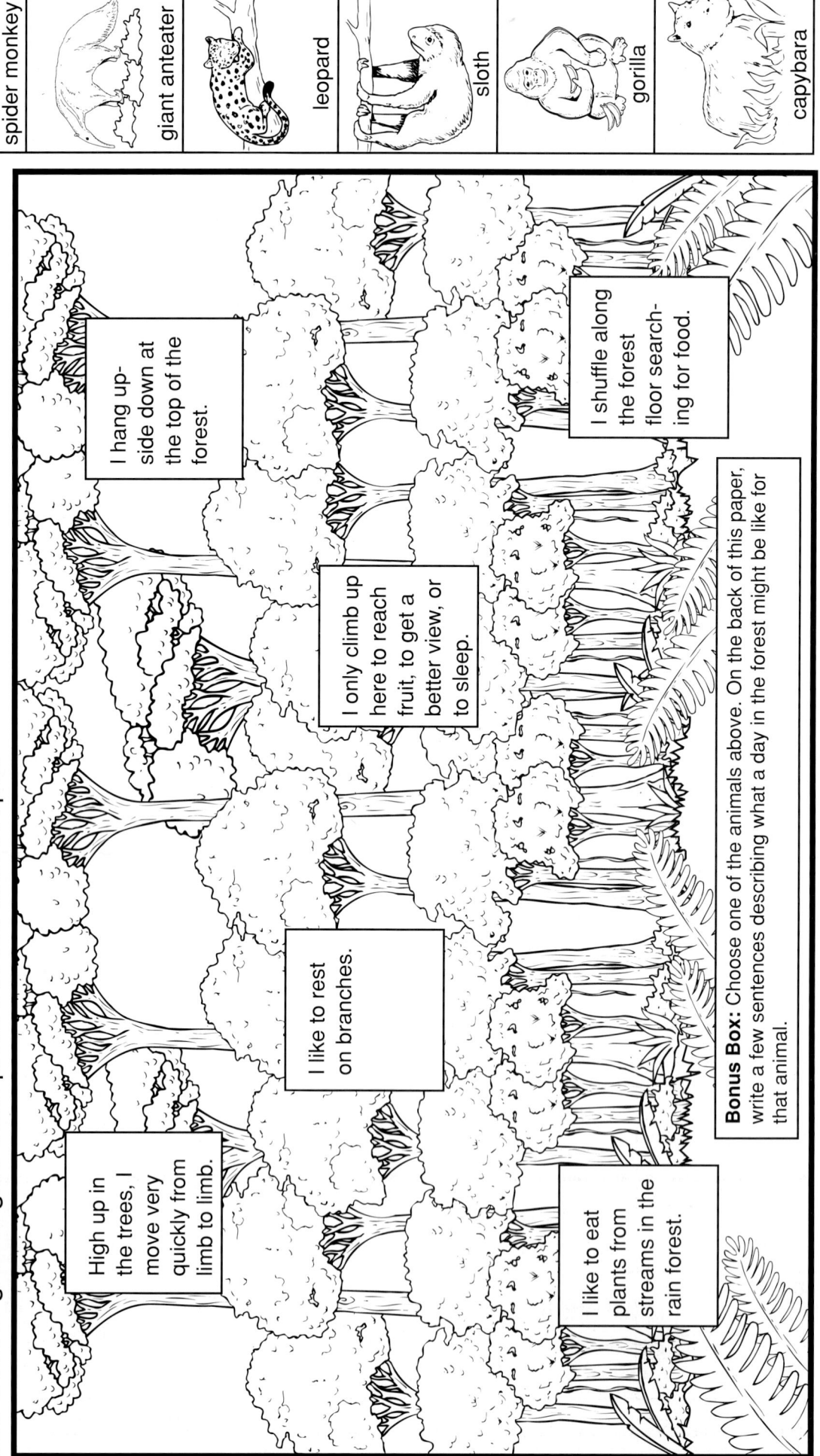

Names _____

Critical thinking, problem solving

Jungle Stats

Below you will find some interesting facts about rain forest animals. Read each fact. Then, with your group, complete the assignment under each fact. Write your answers on the back of this page or on another sheet of paper. After you complete each assignment, have your teacher date and initial in the space provided.

	Fact: Some bush babies can leap 18 feet from branch to branch.
Date completed: Teacher's initials:	**Assignment:** Use masking tape to mark 18 feet either in the hallway or outside on a sidewalk. About how many leaps does it take you to leap 18 feet?
	Fact: Male orangutans weigh up to 265 pounds.
Date completed: Teacher's initials:	**Assignment:** Use a scale to find out how much each person in your group weighs. How many students in your group does it take to weigh as much as a male orangutan?
	Fact: The three-toed sloth is awake for only about six hours each day.
Date completed: Teacher's initials:	**Assignment:** If the sloth wakes up at noon, what time does it go to sleep? Draw two clocks. Have one show when the sloth wakes up, and have the other show when it goes to sleep.
	Fact: Some bats can fly as fast as 35 miles per hour.
Date completed: Teacher's initials:	**Assignment:** Use a map to locate a town about 35 miles from your town. Predict how long you think it might take you to walk 35 miles.
	Fact: The coatimundi's body can be 26 inches long. Its tail can be 27 inches long.
Date completed: Teacher's initials:	**Assignment:** Cut two pieces of yarn: one 26 inches long, and the other 27 inches long. Tape the two pieces together. What is the total length of the coatimundi?

©2000 The Education Center, Inc. • *Investigating Science • Mammals* • TEC1742

Note to the teacher: Group students. Each group will need to have access to the following materials: a yardstick, masking tape, a bathroom scale, a map of your state, and yarn.

27

Grassland Mammals

Take your students on safari and explore the glorious mammals of the grasslands.

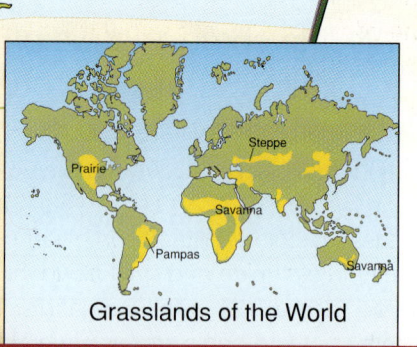

Grasslands of the World

Background for the Teacher

- Grasslands cover one-third of the land on earth.
- Grasslands are also called savannas, pampas, prairies, and steppes.
- *Savannas* are tropical grasslands that cover large portions of Africa and Australia.
- The African savannas are home to the largest, tallest, and fastest land mammals, such as elephants, giraffes, cheetahs, rhinos, hippos, and lions.
- The North American *prairie* is home to hundreds of animal species such as the prairie dog.
- Prairie dogs dig underground tunnels, which help prairie grass grow better.
- Other prairie mammals include coyotes, badgers, weasels, ferrets, bison, and antelope.
- The *pampas* of South America is home to mammals such as the giant anteater, the maned wolf, and the armadillo.
- Grasslands known as *steppes* stretch from Hungary across China.
- Europe's only antelope, the *saiga*, lives in the steppes.

Grassland Field Guides
(Listening Skills, Making a Field Guide)

Reinforce your students' listening skills and introduce them to grassland mammals. Begin by explaining that a *grassland* is an area too wet to be a desert but too dry for trees to grow. Further explain that grasslands cover one-third of the land on earth, and that today most of the grasslands have been turned into farms. Then inform your students that in different parts of the world grasslands are called *savannas, prairies, pampas,* and *steppes.* Using the map shown above, help your students find on a large world map where the four grasslands are located. Next, tell your students that each grassland is teeming with different types of mammals. Inform each student that she is going to create a grassland mammal field guide containing information on some of these mammals. Provide each student with the materials below; then guide her through each step to create her field guide.

Materials: 1 copy each of pages 31 and 32, eight 6" x 9" sheets of paper, one 9" x 12" sheet of colored paper, scissors, crayons, stapler, glue

Steps:
1. Have each student cut out the cards on pages 31 and 32. Then read each description card aloud and ask her to color the mammal that is being described.
2. Next, have the student pair each illustration with its matching description card.
3. Instruct the student to glue each pair of cards onto a 6" x 9" sheet of paper. Have her fold the 9" x 12" sheet of paper in half to make a cover for the guide.
4. Direct the student to stack the eight pages, slip them inside the folded cover, and staple along the fold.
5. Have the student title her booklet "Grassland Mammal Field Guide."

Books to Graze On

An American Safari: Adventures on the North American Prairie by Jim Brandenburg (Walker and Company, 1995)
The Cheetah by Philippe Dupont (Charlesbridge Publishing, 1992)
Grasslands by Alan Collinson (Dillon Press, 1992)
Giraffe Trouble by Jean Craighead George (Disney Press, 1998)
Grassland Mammals by Elaine Landau (Children's Press, 1997)
The Leopard Son: A True Story by Jackie Ball and Kit Carlson (Learning Triangle Press, 1996)
Our Environment (Time Life Student Library) by Karen Kinney (editor) (Time Life Inc., 1999)
What Do We Know About Grasslands? by Brian Knapp (Peter Bedrick Books, 1991)

Research It!
(Research, Using a Graphic Organizer)

Further challenge each student to learn more about one of the mammals in the grassland mammal field guide she created in "Grassland Field Guides" on page 28. Give each student one copy of the graphic organizer on page 33. Then tell each student to choose one mammal from her field guide to research. Provide students with a variety of books on grassland mammals (see booklist on page 28). Then have each student research her chosen mammal and record her findings on page 33. After students have collected and recorded their findings, have each student show the class the colored illustration of her chosen mammal in her field guide and read aloud the information recorded on her graphic organizer. If desired, display all the graphic organizers on a bulletin board titled "Glorious Grassland Mammals."

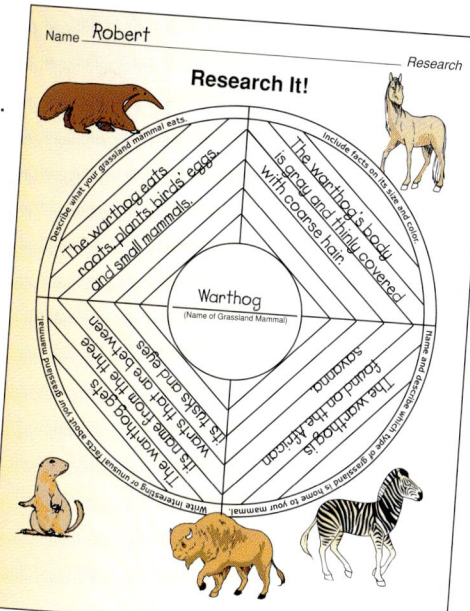

Materials for each student: 1 copy of page 34, 2 small plant pots, potting soil, grass seed, 1 plastic fork, masking tape, permanent marker

Directions:
1. Write on page 34 your hypothesis for why there is always enough grass.
2. Fill both pots with soil.
3. Place a strip of masking tape on each cup, labeling one strip "Grass #1" and the other strip "Grass #2."
4. Sprinkle grass seeds over the top of the soil in both pots and lightly rake the soil using a plastic fork.
5. Lightly water the seeds. Leave the pots in a sunny spot.
6. Water the seeds every other day. Record your observations on page 34.
7. When the grass is about two inches tall (after about two weeks), snip off the tops of Grass #1 with scissors. Leave Grass #2 alone.
8. Continue watering every other day and observe each plant for changes for one week. Record your observations.
9. After three weeks, evaluate your data and observations and write your conclusion on page 34.

Why Is There Always Enough?
(Experiment)

Have you ever wondered why there is always enough grass for all those big grassland mammals to eat? Pose this question to your students and record their answers on the board. Then have your students complete the following experiment to find an answer to the question. Supply each student with the materials at left; then follow the directions to help your students complete the experiment.

After completing the experiment, guide your students in concluding that grassland mammals are merely giving the grass a "haircut." Help students understand that as long as the roots are left undisturbed, the grass will continue to grow, providing a constant source of food for the mammals to eat.

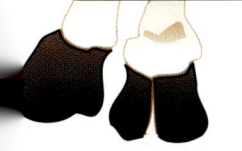

On Guard!
(Game)

Use the following fun and informative game to help your students learn how protective zebras are of their herd members. Begin by explaining to your students that zebras are rather fast mammals and can run up to 40 miles per hour. But even so, sometimes a zebra is caught by a predator. Further explain to your students that to help protect themselves, zebras usually stay together in a herd with at least one member on guard, alert to danger. Tell your students that two zebras will usually stand side by side and face opposite directions, giving them the ability to see in all directions. Their eyes are also on the sides of their heads, giving them a wide range of vision. Now tell your students they are going to play a game called "On Guard," which is similar to the way zebras stand on guard.

To begin, have your students form a large circle. Inform the class that they are a group of lions on the African savanna. Then select two students to be zebra guards in the center of the circle, standing side by side and facing opposite directions. Place a clothespin on the back of each zebra. Tell the class that you are going to be walking swiftly around the circle of lions and will tap one lion on the shoulder. If a student is tapped, she carefully runs up and tries to remove one of the clothespins from the back of a zebra guard. Tell the zebra guards that if one of them can call the approaching student's name before she removes the clothespin, then they are safe and can remain in the circle. If the clothespin is removed, then the lion gets to become a zebra guard and the former zebra joins the circle of lions. Repeat the process until everyone has had a chance to be a zebra guard. Your students will quickly see why zebras are always on guard!

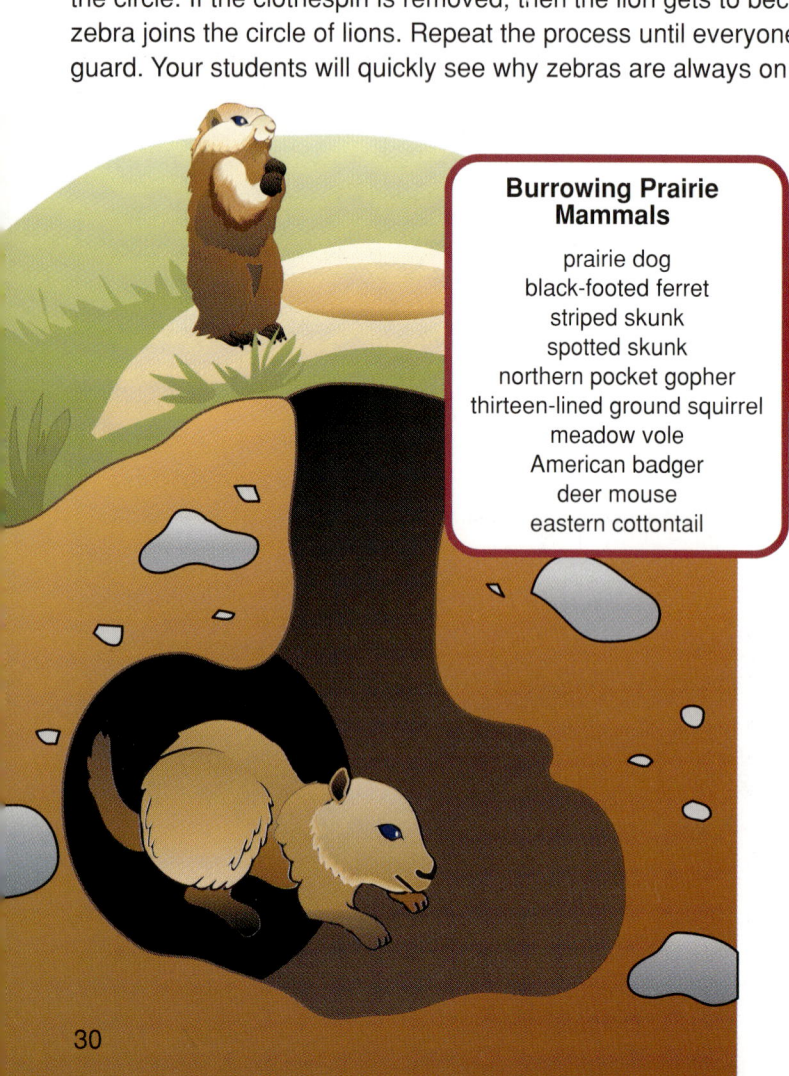

Burrowing Prairie Mammals

prairie dog
black-footed ferret
striped skunk
spotted skunk
northern pocket gopher
thirteen-lined ground squirrel
meadow vole
American badger
deer mouse
eastern cottontail

The Prairie Has a Basement?
(Research)

Did you know that the prairie has a basement? Well, not really, but it does have many mammals that make their homes in burrows and tunnels underground to protect themselves from predators, the summer heat, and harsh winter storms. Share with your students the list of prairie mammals (at left) that make their homes underground. Then provide each student with a copy of page 35. Instruct each student to select one burrowing mammal from the list to research. Have him research the answers to the questions on page 35. Direct the student to record his answers at the top of page 35. Then have the student draw an illustration of the selected mammal's underground home on the bottom of page 35. Have each student share his completed research and illustration with the rest of the class. If desired, post each student's work on a bulletin board titled "Did You Know There Are Mammals Down Below?"

©2000 The Education Center, Inc. • *Investigating Science • Mammals* • TEC1742

Note to the teacher: Use with "Grassland Field Guides" on page 28.

31

Bison (Prairie) I am also called the American buffalo. I'm the largest American animal. I have a large hump on my back and hair that forms a beard under my chin. I'm brownish black on most of my body except for my hind part which is just brown.	**Prairie Dog** (Prairie) I like to dig tunnels underground. These tunnels are where my family and I live. The tunnels also help the prairie grasses grow better. My furry coat is light brown.
Zebra (Savanna) I live in herds. I can run at speeds of up to 40 mph. I have an unusual coat with black-and-white stripes.	**Warthog** (Savanna) I like to eat plants, roots, birds' eggs, and small animals. I have two curved tusks. My body is gray and it's thinly covered with very coarse brownish gray hairs.
Giant Anteater (Pampas) I have very powerful claws that I use to break termite mud castles for food. I have a black band of hair bordered by white bands of hair that begin at my throat and run up to the middle of my back.	**Maned Wolf** (Pampas) I have really long legs that help me see over the tall grass when I'm searching for food (rodents, birds, insects). I have long yellowish orange fur. It grows like a mane down the middle of my back.
Wild Horse (Steppe) I was the earth's last undomesticated horse. I disappeared from the steppes around 1947, but I was bred in captivity and recently put back in my natural home. I have a dark brown mane, a tan coat, and a white underbelly.	**Saiga** (Steppe) I'm Europe's only antelope. I have an unusual bulbous nose that helps warm and moisten cold dry air. I have brown legs and my body and head are light brown.

©2000 The Education Center, Inc. • *Investigating Science • Mammals* • TEC1742

Note to the teacher: Use with "Grassland Field Guides" on page 28.

Name _____ Research

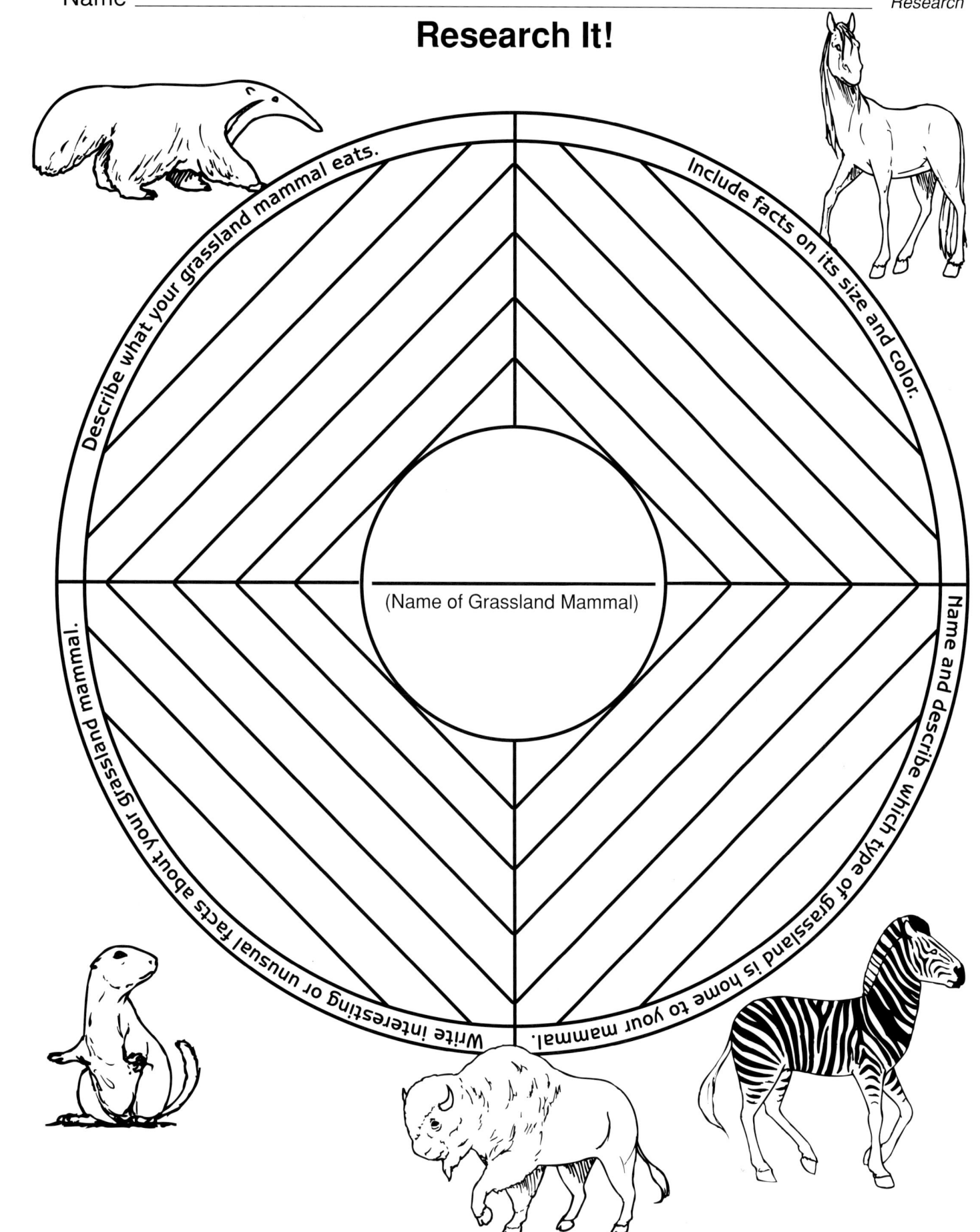

Research It!

Describe what your grassland mammal eats.

Include facts on its size and color.

Name and describe which type of grassland is home to your mammal.

Write interesting or unusual facts about your grassland mammal.

(Name of Grassland Mammal)

©2000 The Education Center, Inc. • Investigating Science • Mammals • TEC1742

Note to the teacher: Use with "Research It!" on page 29.

33

Name _____

Experiment _____

Why Is There Always Enough?

Question: Why is there always enough grass for all the big grazing mammals of the grasslands to eat?

Possible Answer (Hypothesis): _____

What I See (Observations):

Week 1:

Week 2:

Week 3:

What Happened? (Conclusion): _____

Note to the teacher: Use with "Why Is There Always Enough?" on page 29.

Name _____   *Research*

Did You Know There Are Mammals Down Below?

_____
(name of burrowing prairie mammal)

Size: _____

Color: _____

What does it eat? _____

Where does it live? _____

Does it live in a family group? _____

What are its predators? _____

Does it help or hinder the prairie? How? _____

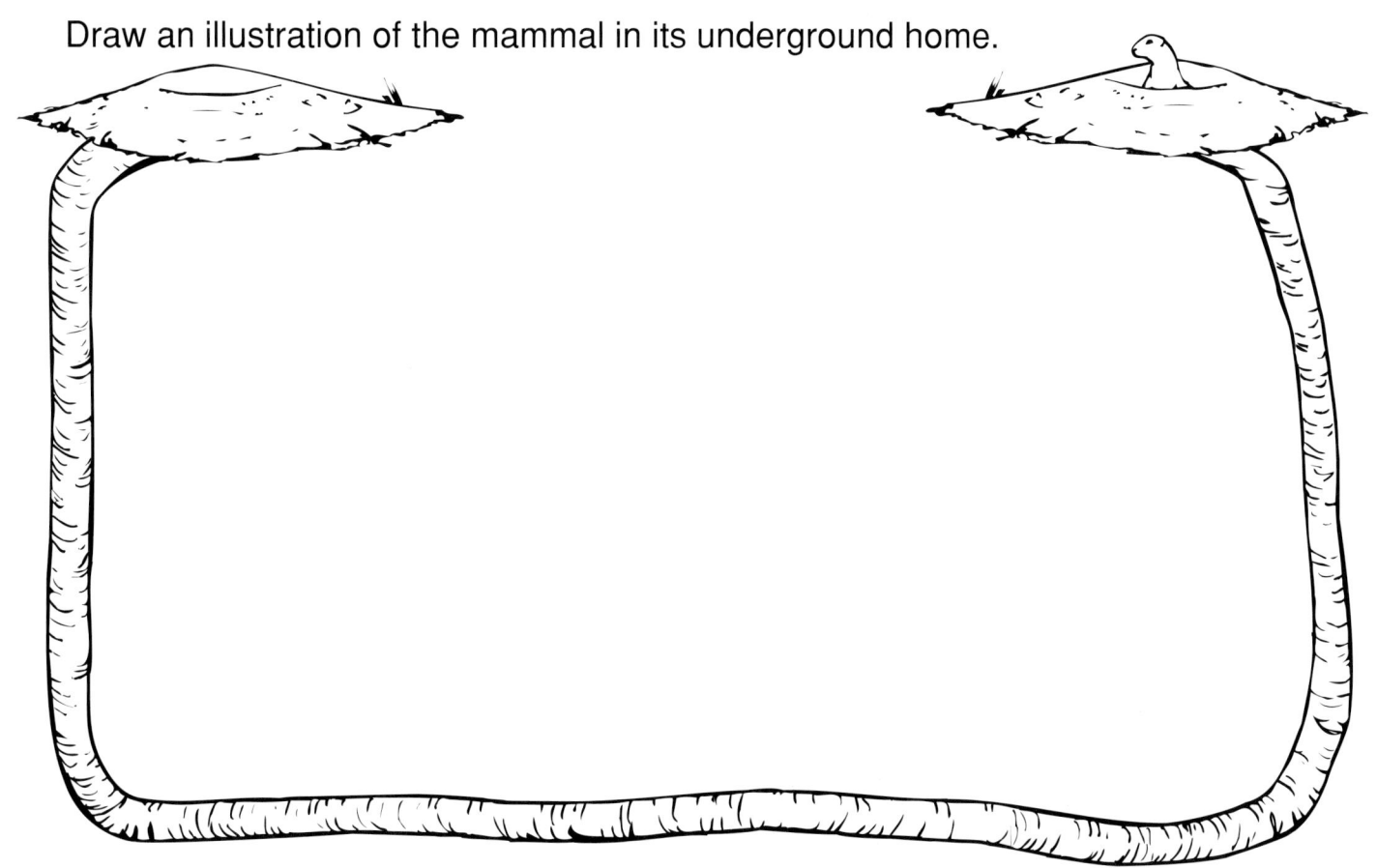

_____

_____

Draw an illustration of the mammal in its underground home.

©2000 The Education Center, Inc. • *Investigating Science • Mammals* • TEC1742

Note to the teacher: Use with "The Prairie Has a Basement?" on page 30.

35

Desert Mammals

Kick it up a notch with these hot activities on desert mammals!

Background for the Teacher

- Deserts are very dry lands where less than ten inches of rain falls each year.
- Most deserts are located near the edges of the tropics. Food and water are often hard to find.
- Desert mammals are able to survive with very little water. The antelope squirrel, for example, gets most of the water it needs from the foods it eats.
- To stay cool, some desert mammals stay in the shade during the hot daylight hours. Other animals, such as the woodrat, burrow into the ground during the day.
- Some desert mammals, such as the cottontail rabbit and the kit fox, come out during the cool evening or early morning hours.
- Some desert mammals, such as the desert hare, have large ears that help them stay cool. The ears act like radiators, allowing excess heat to escape through them.
- Many desert mammals such as mice and hares have small bodies. Their size helps them escape the heat.
- Larger desert mammals include coyotes, camels, dingoes, and mule deer.

Beat the Heat
(Listening, Following Directions)

Shew! It's hot in the desert. Explain to students that one of the greatest challenges that desert mammals face is staying cool. Tell them that desert animals are specially suited for this harsh environment (see the background information on this page). Share with students that many desert mammals—such as the kit fox, bighorn sheep, coyote, and jackrabbit—have light-colored fur. Explain that not only does their fur act as camouflage, it also reflects the sun more effectively than dark fur, keeping them cooler. Tell students that many desert mammals also avoid the sun during the hottest hours of the day. Use the following activity to help your students see how these mammals use their environment to beat the heat.

Give each student a copy of page 39, glue, and scissors. Instruct each student to cut out the six desert illustrations along the bold cut lines. Then instruct the student to listen carefully as you read aloud the first stanza of the poem at the right. After reading the stanza, instruct each student to find the ground squirrel cutout and glue it to the shaded box that is in the correct habitat for the mammal. Continue this process with the remaining five stanzas of the poem. Display the completed scenes on a bulletin board titled "Beat the Heat."

"I'd rather not be so hot," said Cape Ground Squirrel. She stopped in the trail and fluffed her tail and provided her very own shade.

"I'd rather not be so hot," said Desert Bat. He flew into a cave and slept through the day and waited till dark to come out.

"I'd rather not be so hot," said Collared Peccary. She and her family, under the mesquite tree, lazed through the hottest hours.

"I'd rather not be so hot," said Fennec Fox. He dug a big hole and called it a burrow and slept underneath the ground.

"I'd rather not be so hot," said Jackrabbit. She made a nice fur-lined nest in a patch of cactus and slept the day away.

"I'd rather not be so hot," said Coyote. He made his underground burrow near a cavern and settled down for the day.

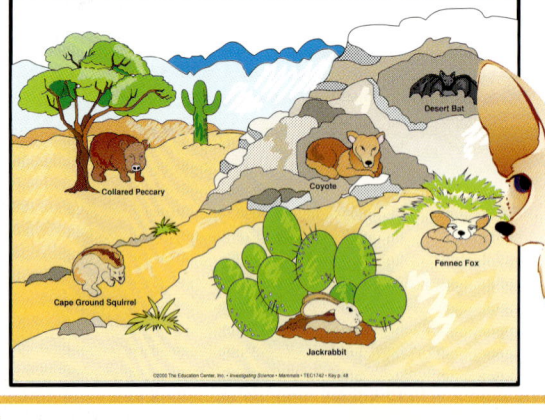

More About Desert Mammals

America's Deserts: Guide to Plants and Animals by Marianne D. Wallace (Fulcrum Publishing, 1996)
Cactus Poems (A Gulliver Green book) by Frank Asch (Harcourt Brace & Company, 1998)
The Desert Alphabet Book by Jerry Pallotta (Charlesbridge Publishing, Inc.; 1994)
The Desert Fox Family Book (Animal Family books) by Hans Gerold Laukel (North-South Books Inc., 1996)
How Jackrabbit Got His Very Long Ears by Heather Irbinskas (Northland Publishing Company, 1994)
In the Desert (Wild Wonders series) by Ann Cooper (Museum of Natural History Press, 1997)

Splitting "Hares"?
(Comparing)

Hop right into this activity comparing the similarities and differences between jackrabbits and rabbits. Begin by explaining to your students that although a jackrabbit and a rabbit look similar and are related, they are not the same—a jackrabbit is a *hare*, not a rabbit. Next, divide your students into groups of three. Supply each group with various resources on jackrabbits and rabbits as well as the materials listed; then guide the group through the directions to complete a jackrabbit-rabbit comparison chart. After each group has completed its chart, discuss as a class the facts that should be in each column of the chart.

Materials for each group:
1 copy of page 40, one 9" x 12" sheet of construction paper, crayons, scissors, glue

Directions:
1. Carefully fold the 9" x 12" sheet of construction paper into three equal sections as shown.
2. Color and cut out the cards at the top of page 40. Glue the "Jackrabbit" card at the top of the left-hand column on the 9" x 12" sheet of construction paper. Then glue the "Both" card at the top of the center column and the "Rabbit" card at the top of the right-hand column.
3. Read the fact cards on page 40.
4. Cut out the fact cards; then glue each card in the correct column.

Materials:
3 thermometers, 1 gardener's trowel, 1 resealable plastic bag, 3 craft sticks painted red

Steps:
1. On a hot sunny afternoon, take the class outside to a dry sandy area.
2. Have a student use the gardener's trowel to dig a hole approximately 12 inches deep. Direct a student to place a thermometer inside the plastic bag, seal it, and then place the bag in the hole. Have a student refill the hole with dirt and mark the spot with a red craft stick.
3. Place the second thermometer in an area on the ground that is in direct sunlight. *(Make sure it's a low traffic area.)* Mark the spot with a red craft stick.
4. Place the third thermometer in a shaded spot on the ground *(in a low traffic area)*. Mark the spot with a red craft stick.
5. After 30 minutes, have one student carefully dig up the buried thermometer and read its temperature. Then have a second and third student locate and read the direct sunlight and shaded thermometers.
6. Return to the class and record the three temperatures on the class prediction chart.
7. Have students compare their predictions to the actual results.

(direct sunlight thermometer = highest temperature; underground thermo-meter = coolest temperature).

Surviving the Sun
(Experiment)

Use the following experiment to help students better understand the intensity of the desert sun and how desert mammals adapt to the sun's harsh rays. Begin the activity by telling your students that many desert mammals spend the hottest part of the day away from direct sunlight. For example, the fennec fox spends the day in its cool underground burrow. Others find refuge in the shade. The xerus, a ground squirrel, even uses its tail to shade itself. Have your students complete the following experiment to see how temperatures differ in the direct sun, in the shade, and underground. Begin by recording on a sheet of chart paper your students' predictions for which location will result in the hottest temperature and which will result in the coolest temperature. Gather the materials listed and follow the steps to complete the experiment with your class. After completing the experiment, refer back to the recorded predictions to see if they were proven true. Then have the class discuss why some desert mammals might choose to dig underground burrows rather than remain out in the sun. Conclude the discussion by explaining that in deserts of the southwestern United States, temperatures can be 110°F with the ground as hot as 160°F. Explain that burrows help desert animals because underground temperatures can be as much as 40°F cooler.

Amazing Desert Mammals
(Making a Class Book)

Book your students on a flight for fact and fiction with this fun and informative bookmaking activity. In advance, enlarge the F pattern shown so that it will be approximately 11" x 8½". Also gather a supply of reference books on desert mammals (see booklist on page 36). Then supply each student with the materials listed below and follow the steps to create your F-shaped "Fact or Fiction" class book. Place the completed booklet in a center or share it with another class. The book will challenge students to distinguish facts about desert mammals from fiction.

Desert Mammals
- xerus
- bat
- jackrabbit
- woodrat
- pocket mouse
- collared peccary
- antelope squirrel
- dromedary camel
- jird
- meerkat
- mule deer
- coati
- fennec fox
- coyote
- kangaroo rat
- bobcat
- cottontail rabbit
- bighorn sheep
- pronghorn
- kit fox
- Bactrian camel
- kulan
- cougar
- ringtail cat

Materials for each student: 2 copies of the enlarged pattern, scissors, crayons

Steps:
1. Assign each student one of the mammals listed in the "Desert Mammals" box.
2. Instruct the student to cut out each pattern and then write the name of the mammal at the top of each pattern as shown.
3. Have the student write a factual statement about his mammal on the upper arm of one pattern just beneath the name of the mammal as shown.
4. Instruct the student to write "Fact" on the lower arm of the pattern and then fold the lower arm in half to hide the answer. (See illustration.)
5. Direct the student to repeat Steps 3 and 4, this time writing a fictional statement on the upper arm and "Fiction" on the lower arm. (Challenge the student to make his fictional statement read as if it might actually be a true statement.)
6. Collect each student's work and compile it into one stack.
7. Trace the enlarged pattern onto two colored sheets of construction paper. Cut out the two patterns. Trim the lower arms of the two patterns to match the length of a folded lower arm in the stack.
8. Place one colored pattern on top of the stack and one on the bottom of the stack; then staple all the pages together along the left-hand side to create a booklet. Title the booklet "Amazing Desert Mammals."

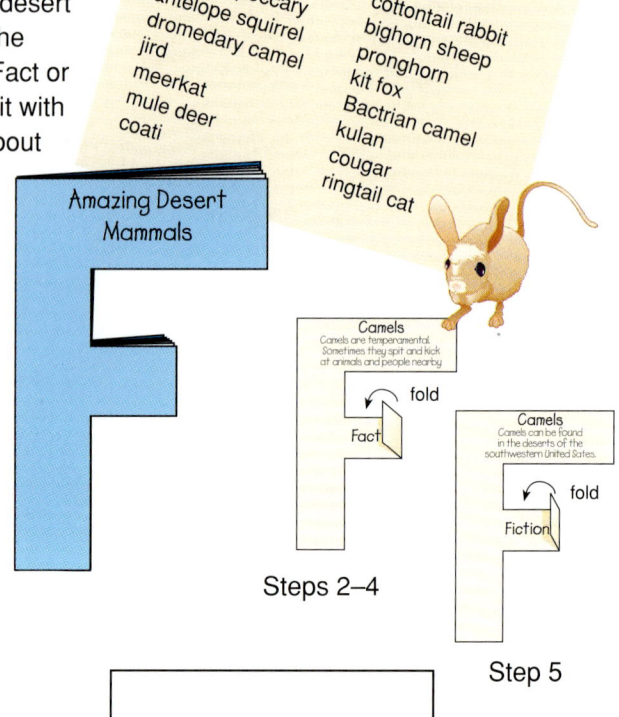

Steps 2–4

Step 5

pattern

Water Hole
(Reading, Research, Writing)

Help your students understand the importance of water to desert mammals by reading *Alejandro's Gift* by Richard E. Albert (Chronicle Books, 1994). Discuss with your class the meaning of this book. (Alejandro is a lonely man who lives in the desert. He works hard to ease his loneliness by trying to draw in the company of desert animals. He gives the animals the water they need and where they need it, but to his surprise, he is the one who receives a gift—companionship.)

Explain to students that after receiving a gift, a thank-you note should be written to the person who gave the gift. Have students imagine that they're desert mammals. Then, from the perspective of a desert mammal, have each student write a thank-you note to Alejandro for the water hole. Make sure the student tells Alejandro about where the mammal spends its days and nights, what it eats, how important the water hole is, and how much it appreciates it.

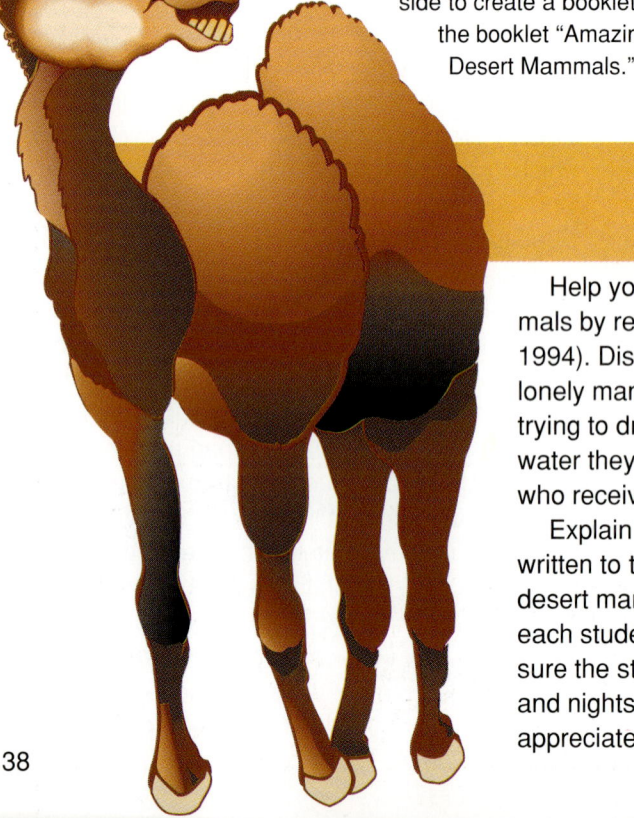

Name _____

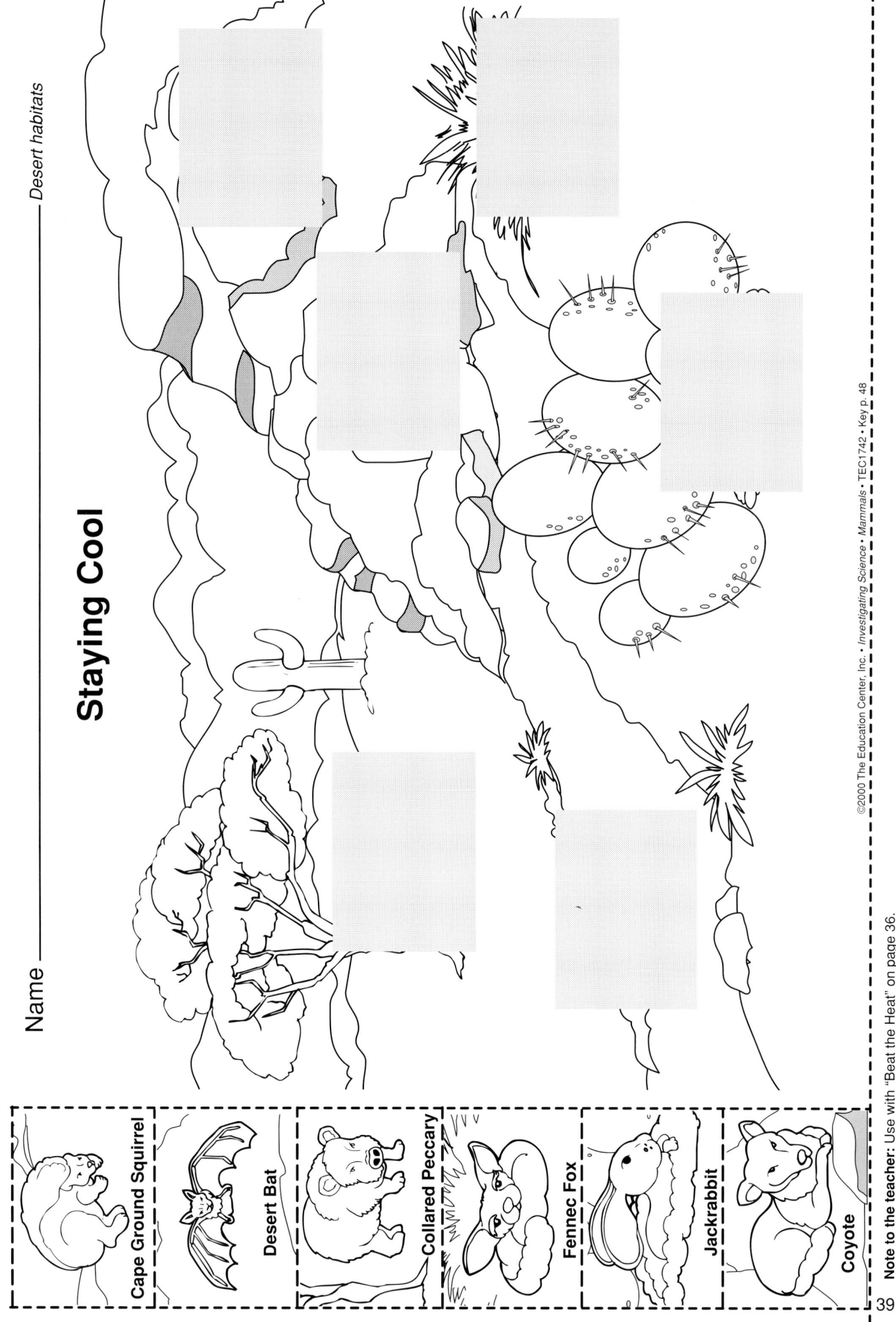

Desert habitats

Staying Cool

| Cape Ground Squirrel | Desert Bat | Collared Peccary | Fennec Fox | Jackrabbit | Coyote |

Note to the teacher: Use with "Beat the Heat" on page 36.

Patterns
Use with "Splitting 'Hares'?" on page 37.

Jackrabbit	Both	Rabbit

I live above ground.	I can reach 15 miles per hour.	My babies are born furless and blind.
I have long ears.	I live alone.	I can reach 30 to 40 miles per hour.
I live in a burrow.	My ears turn for better hearing.	I live in family groups.
I'm a hare.	I have longer legs.	I have shorter legs.
I'm most active at night.	I eat plants.	My babies are born with fur and sight.

Ocean Mammals

This creative collection of activities and reproducibles on ocean mammals will surely be a splash with your students!

Background for the Teacher

- There are four types of sea mammals: *pinnipeds, cetaceans, sirenians,* and *sea otters.*
- Pinnipeds are divided into three groups: eared seals (fur seals and sea lions), earless seals (harbor seals and elephant seals), and walruses.
- *Pinniped* comes from the Latin words meaning "fin-footed."
- Cetaceans are broken into two groups: baleen whales and toothed whales.
- Baleen whales are divided into three groups: right whales, gray whales, and rorquals.
- Baleen whales have hundreds of thin plates instead of teeth to strain *plankton* (tiny sea creatures) from the water.
- Toothed whales are divided into five groups: sperm whales, beaked whales, belugas and narwhals, dolphins and porpoises, and river dolphins.
- Toothed whales have peglike teeth.
- Toothed whales use a process called *echolocation* to locate underwater objects. They listen to echoes produced when objects reflect sounds made by the whale.
- Manatees and dugongs are sirenians.
- Manatees are sometimes called sea cows.
- Sea otters live in the north Pacific Ocean and rarely leave the water.
- Unlike many ocean mammals, sea otters do not have a blubber layer. Instead they have thick fur that holds in air and keeps their skin from getting wet or cold.

Ride the Waves With Ocean Mammals
(Making an Info Booklet)

Help your students catch the wave of learning with the following ocean mammal bookmaking activity! Use this booklet idea to help your students learn facts about the four types of marine mammals. Display a transparency of the information found in the background for the teacher on this page. Then distribute the materials listed and guide each student through the steps below to complete his ocean mammal info booklet. Have your young marine biologists take their ocean mammal info booklets home to share with their families.

Materials needed for each student:
1 copy of page 45
one 9" x 12" sheet of blue construction paper
one 9" x 12" sheet of light blue construction paper
one 6" x 9" piece of light blue construction paper
crayons
ruler
scissors
glue
access to a stapler

Steps:
1. Stack the two 9" x 12" sheets of paper with the darker blue sheet on top. Then slide the top sheet down 1 1/2 inches as shown.
2. Position the 6" x 9" sheet of light blue paper 1 1/2 inches below the top edge of the darker blue sheet as shown.
3. Carefully fold the bottom of the two 9" x 12" sheets up at the base of the 6" x 9" sheet and staple as shown.
4. Cut a wavy edge at the top of each page as shown.
5. Use the background information on the transparency to complete the missing information on page 45.
6. Cut out the four fact blocks and the title block along the bold lines.
7. Glue each fact block and the title block to a separate page as shown.
8. Draw an illustration of each type of marine mammal on the corresponding page.

A Wave of Marine Mammal Books

Humphrey the Lost Whale: A True Story by Wendy Tokuda and Richard Hall (Econo-Clad Books, 1999)
Otter on His Own: The Story of a Sea Otter by Doe Boyle (Soundprints, 1995)
Dolphin's First Day: The Story of a Bottlenose Dolphin by Kathleen Weidner Zoehfeld (Soundprints, 1994)
Raising Ursa by Nicole S. Amato and Carol A. Amato (Barron's Educational Series, Inc.; 1996)
Friends in Deed Save the Manatee by Alison Friesinger (Random House, Inc.; 1998)
The World of Marine Mammals by Adrienne Mason (Orca Book Publishers, 1999)

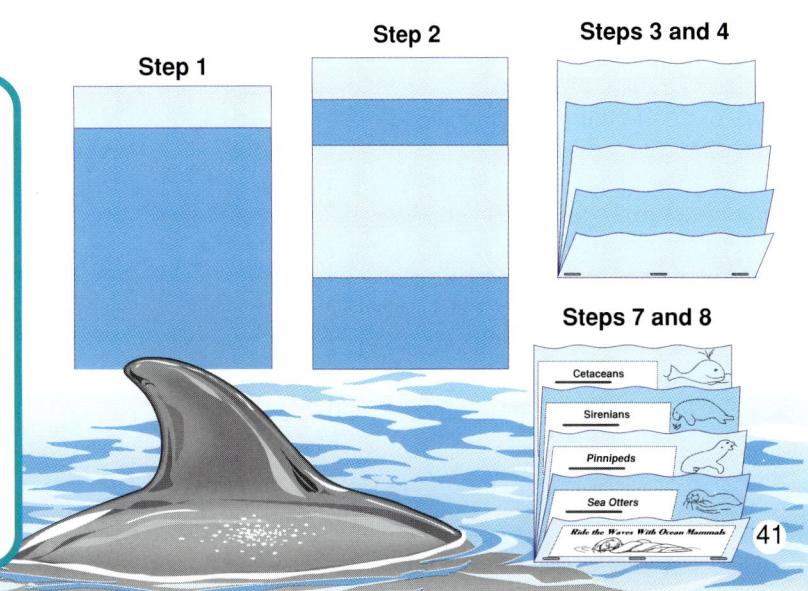

Step 1 **Step 2** **Steps 3 and 4**

Steps 7 and 8

Warming Up With Blubber
(Experiment)

B-r-r-r! How does a baby marine mammal stay warm? A marine mammal mother feeds her young with milk that is very high in fat. This milk helps the baby produce a layer of blubber under the skin which keeps it warm (except sea otters, which have thick fur to keep them warm). As the baby grows, the layer of blubber becomes thicker, providing warmth and protection from the cold ocean waters. Use the following experiment to show your students the importance of blubber to marine mammals. Gather the materials, divide your students into small groups, and follow the steps below. After completing the experiment, have your students conclude what they've learned from it. *(The thicker blubber layer is a better insulator.)*

Materials for each group:
4 quart-size resealable plastic bags
spoon
½ c. and 1½ c. solid vegetable shortening (to be used separately)
2 rubber bands
large dishpan of ice water
paper towels

Steps:
1. Spoon a half cup of shortening into one plastic bag.
2. Turn another plastic bag inside out and place it in the bag with the shortening.
3. Zip the two bags together so the inner bag is sealed to the outer bag.
4. Evenly spread the shortening between the bag layers by squeezing.
5. Repeat Steps 1–4 with the two remaining bags and 1½ cups of shortening.
6. Have one student in each group place one hand inside each bag. Secure each bag onto the student's hand by placing a rubber band around the opening of each bag.
7. Instruct the student to dip both hands into the ice water and determine which hand is kept warmer. *(The hand in the blubber mitt containing 1½ cups of shortening will feel warmer.)*
8. Repeat Steps 6 and 7 with each group member.

Marine Mammals on the Move
(Map Skills, Migration)

Introduce ocean mammal migration to your students with this map activity. Explain to students that many ocean mammals, such as right whales and fur seals, *migrate*. Ocean mammals migrate to different parts of the ocean to find warmer waters, locate food, and give birth to babies. Many follow the same migration path from year to year. Give each student a copy of page 46. Have him use the key at the bottom of the reproducible to color the migration routes of gray whales, fur seals, blue whales, and right whales. After the maps are complete, have each student locate the marine mammal homes on a globe or map and then use his fingers to trace the migration paths.

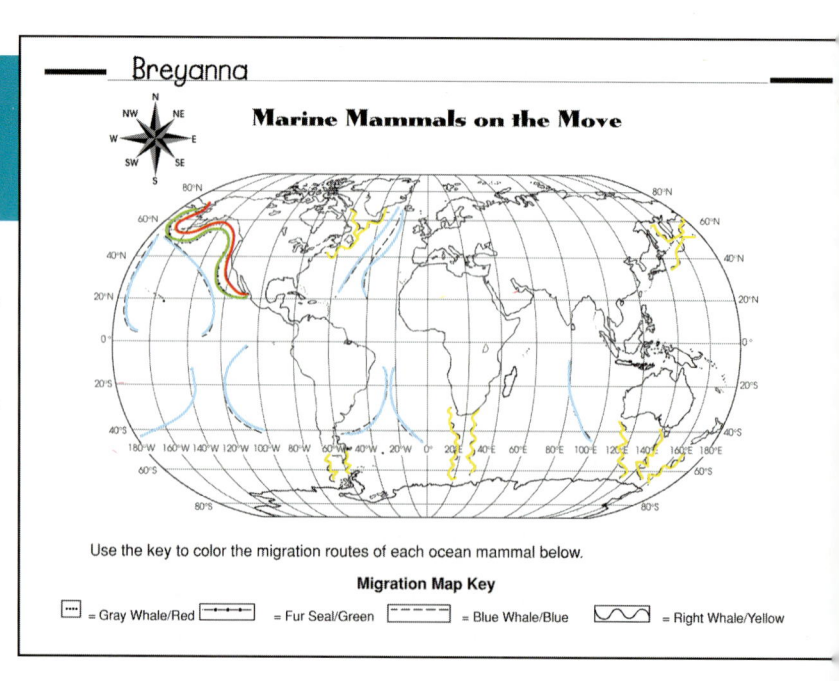

Combing the Ocean
(Demonstration)

Some of the largest whales do not have teeth. Instead they have *baleen,* hundreds of thin plates (much like the material of human fingernails) that hang down from the whale's upper jaw. In order to eat, a baleen whale takes in large amounts of water, using the baleen to filter out food (plankton). Use the following two simple activities to demonstrate to your students how baleen whales catch and eat their food. Gather the materials listed and follow the steps to complete each demonstration. Bon appétit!

Activity 1

Materials needed:
a large plastic dishpan
several plastic hair combs
water
parsley flakes

Steps:
1. Fill the dishpan with water; then sprinkle parsley flakes on top of the water. Explain to your students that the parsley flakes represent plankton in the ocean water.
2. Show your students a hair comb. Explain that the comb represents the baleen that hangs from a whale's jaw.
3. Use the comb to rake through the water. Have your students observe what happens *(the comb filters some of the parsley flakes from the water just as the baleen filters plankton from the ocean water).*
4. Have students take turns using the comb to rake through the water to experience the process for themselves.

Activity 2

Materials for each student:
1 small paper cup
a tablespoon
a half teaspoon
water
cake sprinkles

Steps:
1. Instruct each student to spoon one tablespoon of water into her cup; then add one-half teaspoon of plankton (cake sprinkles).
2. Direct the student to sip the water and sprinkles without swallowing.
3. Have her use her tongue to carefully push the water out through her teeth, keeping her lips closed to make the water stay in her mouth.
4. Have the student swallow the water; then eat the plankton (sprinkles) left on the backs of her teeth.

Bouncing Sounds
(Experiment)

Ever wonder how some marine mammals find food in the dark waters of the ocean? Whales, dolphins, sea lions, and seals use *echolocation* to find objects in the water. The animal produces sounds that travel through the water. The sounds echo back when they bounce off an object. The animal is able to tell how far away the object is and in what direction it's located. The animal can tell what kind of object is in its path according to the type of echo it hears. Use the following simple activity to show your students how echolocation works. Gather a class supply of small balls (tennis balls work nicely). Take students into the hallway or outside. Give each student a ball and have her face a wall so that she is about five feet away from it. Tell each student to pretend that she is a whale, dolphin, sea lion, or seal. Then, on your signal, have each student toss her ball toward the wall. Explain that this represents the initial sound sent out by the animal. Instruct the child to observe what happens once the ball hits the wall *(it bounces back toward her).* Explain that this represents the sound waves sent by the animal bouncing off an object and returning to the animal. Have the student repeat this process from different distances and observe the various "echoes"!

Terrific Training
(Listening, Following Directions)

Many toothed whales, such as killer whales and dolphins, are highly intelligent. In captivity, dolphins are eager to learn tricks by responding to simple hand motions or sound signals. When a correct response is received, the animal is rewarded. It looks easy, but is it? See if your students can remember ten simple responses when you give them a particular signal. After your students perform a desired action, provide positive verbal reinforcement by saying, "Good job, super seals," "Way to go, wonderful whales," or "Well done, dandy dolphins." When all ten signals and responses listed below are learned, reward your students with a fishy treat of Goldfish® crackers.

Teacher Signal	Student Response
Clap once.	Sit up straight.
Raise right hand.	Fold hands on desk.
Raise left hand.	Blink eyes.
Point one finger.	Put one hand on head.
Extend arm with palm down.	Stand up.
Snap fingers twice.	Turn to the right.
Clap twice.	Turn to the left.
Nod head.	Touch knees.
Twirl hand in a circular motion.	Put hands over ears.
Pull an earlobe.	Smile!

Save Our Marine Mammal Friends
(Critical Thinking, Art)

Help your students share a sea of information concerning ocean pollution and its effects on marine mammals by creating warning posters. Explain to your students that many marine mammals die each year because of human carelessness. Trash (especially plastics) left on beaches or dumped in the ocean causes many animals to get sick and die. Further explain that the animals mistake plastic trash as food or playthings and get entangled in plastic bags, packing straps, fishing lines, and abandoned or lost commercial fishing nets. Share with your students that oil spills also have dangerous effects on marine mammals. For example, oil can clog the baleen fibers in a whale's mouth, preventing it from being able to catch food. Oil penetrates the fur of sea otters, causing them to lose their natural insulation.

Empower your students to help others in your school and community learn about the dangers of pollution to ocean mammals by having each student create a warning poster. (In advance, collect trash such as six-pack rings, net, plastic bags, empty motor oil containers, etc.) Provide each student with a 12" x 18" sheet of construction paper and crayons or markers. Instruct the student to create a poster warning others of the dangers of ocean pollution. Have each student add 3-D effects to his poster by attaching some of the collected trash to it. Display the posters along a hallway to help educate other students about the effects of pollution on ocean mammals.

Trashing the Sea Isn't Cool. The Ocean's Not a Dump!
Keep these out of our oceans:
Plastic Bags
Fishing Line
Six-Pack Rings

Ride the Waves With Ocean Mammals

Cetaceans

The two types of cetaceans are

_____ and _____.

Baleen whales do not have _____.

Toothed whales use _____ to find their food.

Pinnipeds

Three types of pinnipeds are

_____, _____, and _____.

The name *pinniped* comes from Latin words meaning _____.

Sirenians

The two types of sirenians are

_____ and _____.

Manatees are sometimes called _____.

Sea Otters

Sea otters do not have a layer of _____.

Sea otters stay warm because of their _____.

Note to the teacher: Use with "Ride the Waves With Ocean Mammals" on page 41.

Name _____

Marine Mammals on the Move

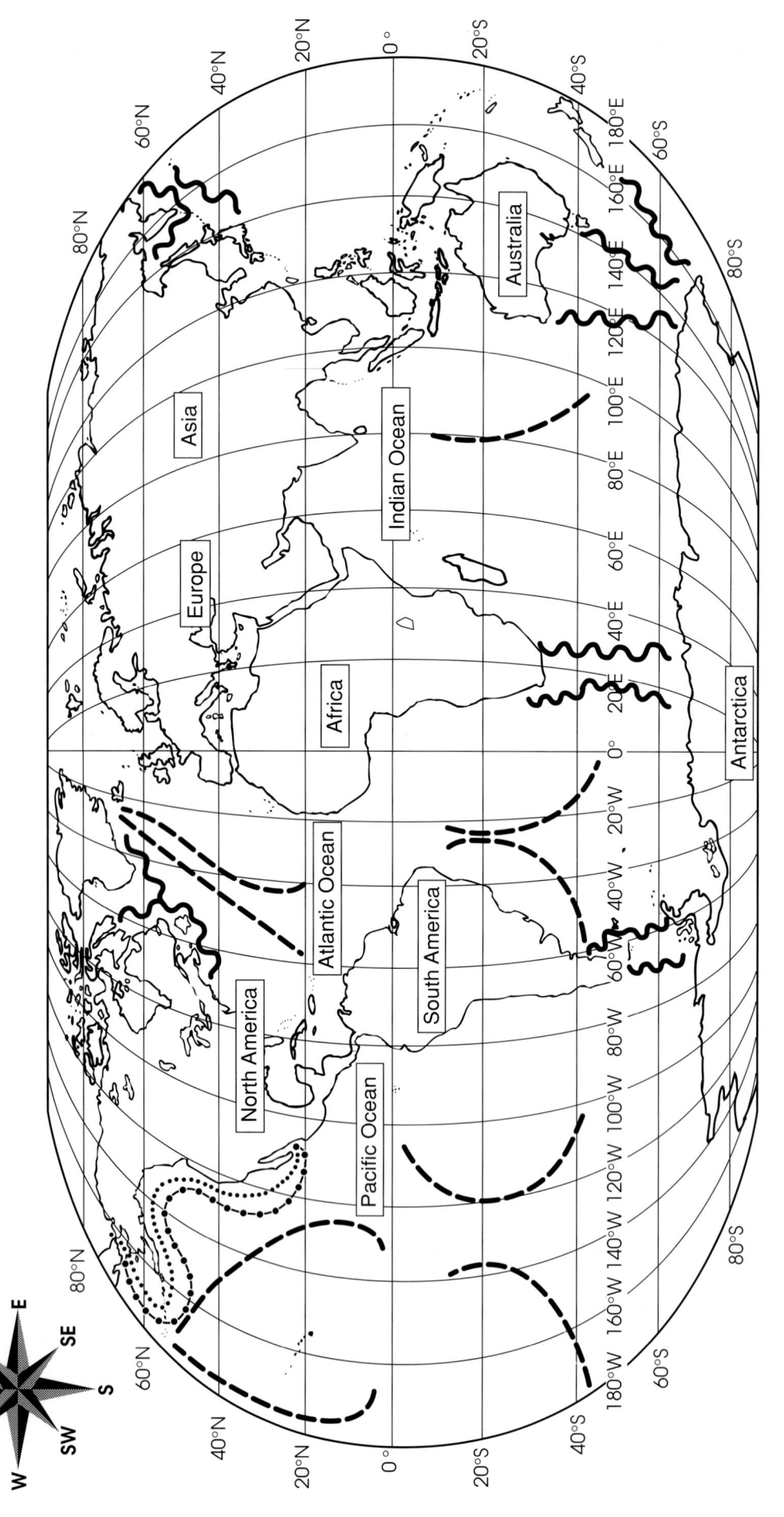

Use the key to color the migration routes of each ocean mammal below.

Migration Map Key

⋯⋯ = Gray Whale/Red

▬▬ = Fur Seal/Green

- - - - = Blue Whale/Blue

〰〰 = Right Whale/Yellow

Note to the teacher: Use with "Marine Mammals on the Move" on page 42.

©2000 The Education Center, Inc. • *Investigating Science • Mammals* • TEC1742 • Key p. 48

Name_____ Reading a graph

Comparing Marine Mammals

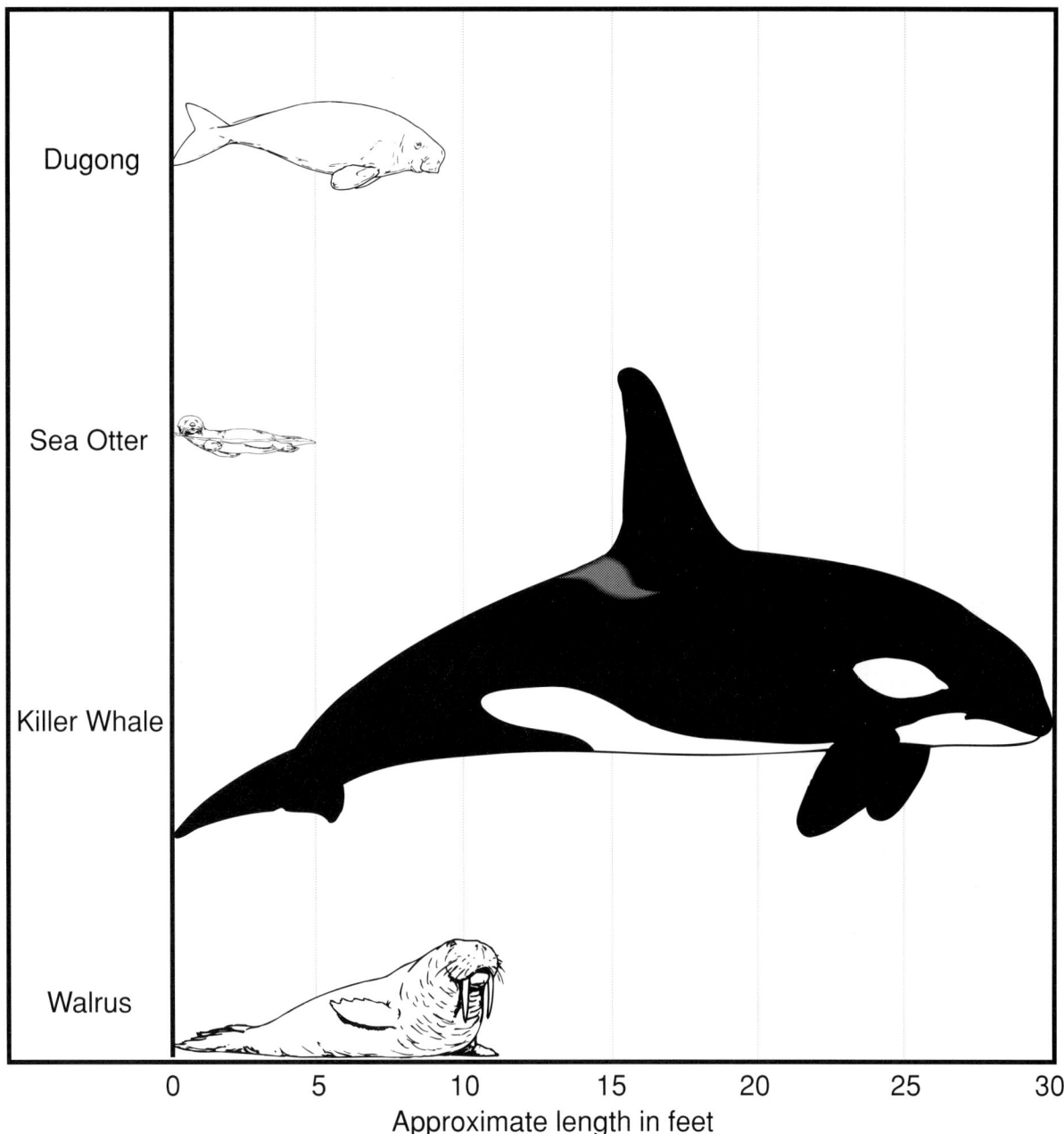

Dugong

Sea Otter

Killer Whale

Walrus

0   5   10   15   20   25   30
Approximate length in feet

Use the graph to answer the questions.

1. Which animal is 12 feet long? _____

2. Which animal is shorter than a walrus and longer than a sea otter? _____

3. Which animal is 30 feet long? _____

4. How many feet longer is the killer whale than the dugong? _____

5. List the animals from shortest to longest. _____

_____

©2000 The Education Center, Inc. • Investigating Science • Mammals • TEC1742 • Key p. 48

Answer Keys

Page 9
It Must Be a Mammal

	Does it have hair or fur?	Does it have a backbone?	Does it have two pairs of limbs?	Does it drink milk from its mother?
horse	X	X	X	X
grizzly bear	X	X	X	X
earthworm				
elephant	X	X	X	X
rabbit	X	X	X	X
spider	X			
kangaroo	X	X	X	X
chicken		X	X	
grasshopper				
human	X	X	X	X

Bonus Box answer: *Accept any reasonable explanation for why each animal listed is not a mammal.*
earthworm—An earthworm has no limbs.
spider—A spider has more than two pairs of limbs.
chicken—A chicken hatches from an egg.
grasshopper—A grasshopper is an insect.

Page 13
(Answers for "Home, Sweet Home" chart.)
Note: Some animals listed may live in more than one type of home.

	Wooded Area	Den	Nest	Burrow	Tunnel	Hollow Tree	Lodge
Bear		✓					
Porcupine						✓	
Skunk		✓					
Fox		✓					
Squirrel			✓				
Chipmunk				✓			
Rabbit				✓			
Marmot				✓			
Woodchuck		✓		✓			
Mole					✓		
Mouse				✓			
Deer	✓						
Beaver							✓
Opossum						✓	
Raccoon						✓	
Marten						✓	
Otter		✓		✓			
Muskrat				✓			

Page 26
(rainforest image with labels: spider monkey, sloth, leopard, gorilla, capybara, giant anteater)

Bonus Box answer: Answers will vary.

Page 39
Staying Cool
(desert scene with labels: Collared Peccary, Coyote, Desert Bat, Cape Ground Squirrel, Fennec Fox, Jackrabbit)

Page 40

Jackrabbit	Both	Rabbit
I live above ground.	I have long ears.	I live in a burrow.
I'm a hare.	I'm most active at night.	I can reach 15 miles per hour.
I have longer legs.	My ears turn for better hearing.	I have shorter legs.
I live alone.	I eat plants.	I live in family groups.
My babies are born with fur and sight.		My babies are born furless and blind.
I can reach 30 to 40 miles per hour.		

Page 45
Cetaceans
The two types of cetaceans are **toothed whales** and **baleen whales**.
Baleen whales do not have **teeth**.
Toothed whales use **echolocation** to find their food.

Sirenians
The two types of sirenians are **manatees** and **dugongs**.
Manatees are sometimes called **sea cows**.

Pinnipeds
Three types of pinnipeds are **seals**, **sea lions**, and **walruses**.
The name *pinniped* comes from Latin words meaning **fin-footed**.

Sea Otters
Sea otters do not have a layer of **blubber**.
Sea otters stay warm because of their **thick fur**.

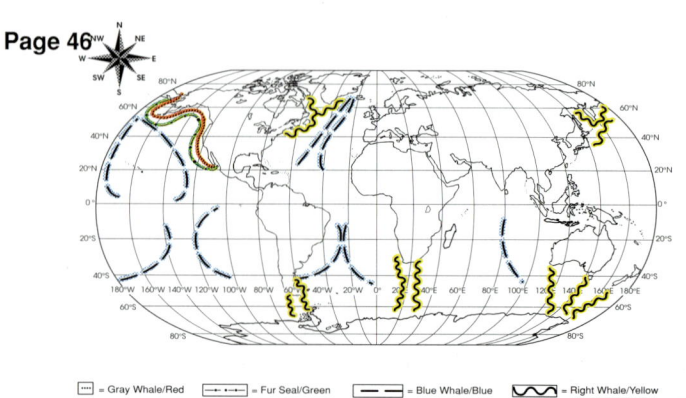

Page 46
(world map showing whale migration routes)
⋯ = Gray Whale/Red   ⋯ = Fur Seal/Green   — = Blue Whale/Blue   ∿ = Right Whale/Yellow

Page 47
1. walrus
2. dugong
3. killer whale
4. 21 feet
5. sea otter, dugong, walrus, killer whale